The Seven Noses
of Soho

The Seven Noses
of Soho

And 191 Other Curious Details
from the Streets of London

Jamie Manners

Michael O'Mara Books Limited

First published in Great Britain in 2015 by
Michael O'Mara Books Limited
9 Lion Yard
Tremadoc Road
London SW4 7NQ

A CIP catalogue record for this book is available from the British Library.

Papers used by Michael O'Mara Books Limited are natural, recyclable products made from wood grown in sustainable forests. The manufacturing processes conform to the environmental regulations of the country of origin.

ISBN: 978-1-78243-461-0 in hardback print format
ISBN: 978-1-78243-462-7 in ebook format

1 2 3 4 5 6 7 8 9 10

Jacket design and illustrations by James Nunn

Designed and typeset by Envy Design Ltd

Printed and bound by CPI Group (UK) Ltd, Croydon, CR0 4YY

www.mombooks.com

To Charlie

Contents

Introduction

'Of course, London is a big place, it's a very big place, Mr Shadrack. A man could lose himself in London.' – Billy Fisher (Tom Courtenay), *Billy Liar* (1963)

When a man is tired of London, he will be very, very tired of hearing that old line by Dr Johnson. Fortunately, for those who know where to look, antidotes do exist.

Recently I was on a flight to Gatwick. England was unusually cloudless, and we could see far and wide as the captain readied our descent. When the plane turned in preparation, London came into view in the middle distance. Having spent my whole adult life in London, I had never seen anything like it. We were just distant enough that London could be seen from end to end, a sight that I had never dreamed possible (unless from space or in a CGI-heavy film). The entire city was a monstrously sized saucer, with upward ridges around its edges but otherwise smooth and level, perhaps dipping a little at the centre. We were just close enough that I could identify some of London's tallest landmarks; the Shard, the Gherkin and the pyramid peak of Canary Wharf all stood out, although none looked taller than a grain of rice. The anecdote is banal, but it illustrates one of London's strengths: the ability to continually surprise those who know the city well. Patrick Hamilton wrote of 20,000 streets under the sky; today, there are 60,000 within a six-mile radius of Charing Cross. This modest and subjective compendium of one person's findings could never be comprehensive because there is so much of London waiting to be discovered that a single volume will barely scratch its surface.

Among the great historic cities of the world, London is particularly rich because it has no single unifying style. Wren hoped to impose one as the city rebuilt itself after the Great Fire, but London was too attached to its medieval street plan. Rather than one man's vision, this city is a result of thousands of compromises, accidents and moments of improvisation. Every generation leaves another its mark, adding new chapters to London's story. Paris or Venice may be more beautiful, but a city planned to perfection is a city that resists change and struggles to adapt. Like the teeming crowds who live and work there, the streets of London have always shown a tumult of different influences. Each age is still present, and competes for your attention. Walk around

London and you will not just go from place to place, you will travel through the centuries.

The chameleon nature of the London skyline means that this book cannot help but be dated. Some of the best things in it are currently living a very precarious existence and may soon be gone. Revisit London in 2035 and there will be many marvellous new things at which to wonder, and no doubt a far greater number of dreadful ones. A plot of London land will be written over as many times as a classroom blackboard.

Continual change can be wearing on the nerves, and the direction in which London is currently heading is a grave concern. Written when war was the existential threat, Noël Coward's 'London Pride' celebrated neither the costermongers of Covent Garden's vegetable market nor the society ladies of Park Lane, but the variety signified by their juxtaposition. The latter are now expelling the former. Both property speculation and the spread of gentrification have rendered London's traditionally cheap areas very expensive. If only the very rich can live here, this great city will lose its vitality, its ebullience and – wherever they happened to be born – its true Londoners. If the drive to acquire as much money as possible supplants every other concern, the incredible stories to be found within London will dry up altogether. What shall it profit a city if it gains every billionaire in the world and loses its soul?

Fortunately London has 2,000 years of history behind it. Spreading far beyond its original city walls, London has swallowed up countless villages and towns, each with its own identity and its own story. This book will not describe the iconic London sights, such as Big Ben or St Paul's, that are well covered elsewhere. It will focus on the streets of London, and attempt to show that they contain exhibits just as intriguing and enlightening as the treasures of the British Museum and National Gallery. Even commonplace pieces of street furniture such as letterboxes or lampposts reveal unexpected dramas. These small details are what has given London a human face and made millions fall for it.

This book is populated with tigers and flamingos, Roman emperors and Crusader knights, elves and devils, dead rock stars and Soviet spies. Its tales include the temporary Belgian village in the heart of England, a cul-de-sac in Holborn that is officially part of Cambridgeshire, three west London streets that seceded from Britain and a series of riots over a dog statue. From Wren to Renzo Piano and Bazalgette to Banksy, it showcases some of the curiosities that hide in plain sight, and demonstrates that the story of London is the story of the world. Next time you are heading for your rush-hour train, why not turn away from the stampeding crowds and take a look around: you may find some London stories of your own. When you've seen how big this city is, you realize that the stories are in infinite supply and being added to every day.

Central Line

Running from the well-heeled suburbs of the west to the mock-Tudor heartlands of Essex is the Central line. It takes in west London, the West End, the City, the East End and the new Olympic sites at Stratford. In 1900, it opened as the egalitarian 'twopenny Tube', running from Shepherd's Bush to Bank. Mark Twain was a passenger on its inaugural journey. To the west of Holborn is a disused station called British Museum. During World War II, the tunnels between Leytonstone and Gants Hill were used as a secret factory for aircraft components.

Bank and St Paul's bring you to two of the most important sites in the City of London, which for so many centuries was the entirety of London. When we visit European cities, we tend to stick to sightseeing in the historic centre, yet Londoners are often cut off from the inheritance of their own *centro storico*. The City is a living museum of treasures, but the only people going there habitually are the ones moving around imaginary money in computers and those who make their sandwiches. When Wren's churches were under threat, T.S. Eliot wrote that they gave 'to the business quarter of London a beauty which its hideous banks and commercial houses have not quite defaced . . . the least precious redeems some vulgar street'.

HOLLAND PARK

REMAINS OF HOLLAND HOUSE
Holland Park, W8 6LU

The Grand Tour of the eighteenth and nineteenth centuries was a sort of gap year for aristocrats. Once in Italy, they would feast on the remnants of the Roman world, and often develop a taste for ruins. Fragments of ancient castles, temples and arches were decreed 'picturesque', and perhaps gave the emergent British Empire a titillating preview of its own annihilation. Our own picturesque ruin can be found at the centre of Holland Park, courtesy of the Luftwaffe. Built in 1605, Holland House (originally Cope House) was a substantial stately home, used by royals and Roundheads alike. In the early nineteenth century, the 3rd Lord Holland established a salon that became the unofficial Whig headquarters; it was from here that the Great Reform Act of 1832 was plotted. A distinguished CV was curtailed in 1940, when the house was struck by twenty-two German bombs in a single night. Today, it looks as though three-quarters of Holland House is missing, which is indeed the case. The east wing remains intact, along with a little of the ground floor. A three-sided, recessed portico walkway, with round arches and fleurs-de-lis garlanding its roof, traces where the façade once stood. Currently a youth hostel, the east wing features gables and an attractive bay window, and at its rear stands a solitary turret from the main house. Amputated from the great house it once served, the walkway could now be a theatre prop; the mutilated fragments seem as forlorn as severed limbs scattered across a battlefield.

KYOTO GARDEN
100 Holland Park Avenue, W11 4UA

The historic city of Kyoto was the Japanese capital for over a millennium. Today it is home to some 400 Shinto shrines and 1,600 Buddhist temples, including the Temple of the Golden Pavilion. Londoners wishing to indulge in quiet contemplation need not endure the twelve-hour flight to Japan, for at the secluded heart of Holland Park sits the Kyoto Garden. To mark 1992's Japan Festival in London, a prominent Japanese designer landscaped this garden in accordance with Zen principles. Koi carp dart around the pool's stone lanterns, and peacocks strut across the lawns. In autumn the diminutive maple trees display leaves of red and gold. Centre-stage is a waterfall, cascading into the pond over tiers of carefully placed rocks, with a staggered wooden bridge across the pond offering the best views. It all makes an atmospheric replica. A new section was added in 2012 in thanks for the United Kingdom's support after the nuclear accident at Fukushima.

TILES
Debenham House, 8 Addison Rd, Kensington, W14 8DJ

An ageing prostitute is haunted by the death of her daughter. Across town, a lunatic waif who is the daughter's double lives alone in a ten-bedroom house after the death of her own mother (who in turn looked just like the prostitute) and one day the pair meet on the top deck of a No. 27 bus . . . If Joseph Losey's 1968 film *Secret Ceremony* sounds a cul-de-sac of nonsense, that's because it is, but something about this nasty, psychotic film stays with the viewer. That something is probably the film's inspiration and true star, the extraordinary house at 8 Addison Rd. Sometimes called Peacock House, it was built in 1907 for the owner of the famed department store (Debenhams, not Peacocks). The startling exterior is clad in tiles of lustrous blue above green, framed by rows of cream terracotta. Art nouveau looked to nature, and these colours were chosen accordingly; the tiles match the sky and gardens, making the house seem a transparent spectre. With sensible stucco-fronted houses for neighbours, Debenham House stands out as a cabaret drag act. The exotic interior boasts an inner dome of Byzantine mosaics: gold, Greek lettering and zodiac animals straight from Ravenna. The house is not open to the public, but one can take in its exterior from the street and peek through the gate down an arcaded walkway.

QUEENSWAY

THE ELFIN OAK
Kensington Gardens, W2 2UH

This whimsical creation is not to everyone's taste, but it should light up the faces of the young and the young-at-heart alike. The Elfin Oak is a 900-year-old tree. In 1928 it was moved from Richmond Park to Kensington Gardens, and in 1930 the artist Ivor Innes picked up his carving knife to create a community of little people living on and within the tree. Some characters help each other to climb up the tree, some sit astride protruding knobs of wood, and some shelter in hollows. The fantasy includes elves, gnomes, princesses, witches, animals, people dining around a giant flat toadstool, and even a well-stocked elf library where a literary pixie sits with a pot of quill pens. The detail, from varied facial expressions to neckerchiefs, belt buckles and musical instruments, is accomplished. The artwork of Pink Floyd's *Ummagumma* album shows David Gilmour posing before the tree. The Elfin Oak was showing signs of deterioration when Spike Milligan intervened, leading to its restoration in 1996 and Grade II listing. Sited beside the café at the entrance to the Princess Diana Memorial Playground, it is now protected by a cage. Complementing the oak is the Peter Pan statue located south of the Italian Gardens.

23–24 LEINSTER GARDENS
W2 3AN

Appearances can be deceiving. In the salubrious streets to the north of Hyde Park is a row of terraces, chiefly housing hotels. Take a closer look and you will realize that two houses are hollow façades covering a blank space. The original houses at this address were demolished to make way for Underground train tracks and replaced with a phantom façade that mimics the Henry VIII Hotel next door. The first-floor windows are framed by Corinthian columns, pediments and balconies, some of which even have potted bay trees to match those of the hotel. Decoration gradually lessens until the servants' quarters on the top floor. There are a couple of hints that all is not what it seems, such as pristine grey paint in lieu of glass panes, and the joints in the front doors being painted over, but the effect is uncanny and slightly eerie. If this all seems hard to fathom, walk to Porchester Terrace where, like Dorothy confronting the Wizard, you will see nothing except a few iron beams propping up the impostor.

MARBLE ARCH

10 HYDE PARK PLACE
Tyburn Convent, W2 2LJ

In Porto, the one-metre gap between the baroque twin churches of Carmo and Carmelitas contains a little house, built to prevent illicit liaisons between the nuns and monks. It is tempting to envisage a similar story for 10 Hyde Park Place, itself attached to a convent and London's smallest house at just 106 cm wide. The façade curves towards the convent and matches its red brick, making it look like a mere appendage, so it's a surprise that No. 10 should

have its own number. It was originally a house in its own right, built in 1805 to prevent access to St George's graveyard. At the time, medical schools would pay a handsome fee for fresh corpses and many took to the grisly career of bodysnatching. The convent owns the property now, and the physical similarities to the parent building date from restoration after the Blitz. Halfway down the chapel wall, a door opens onto a tiny balcony that would make an excellent outdoor pulpit should the nuns wish to harangue the frisbee players of Hyde Park.

CHANCERY LANE

OSTLER'S HUT
The Honourable Society of Lincoln's Inn, WC2A 3TL

The four Inns of Court around Fleet St and Chancery Lane are London's equivalent of Oxbridge colleges. In the midst of the city's mayhem, they are hermetically sealed worlds with splendid old buildings, chapels, cloisters and gardens. These tranquil surroundings are where London's barristers ply their trade. The gardens at Lincoln's Inn were the venue for the first performance of *A Midsummer Night's Dream*, and across the lawn from the great library is the smallest listed building in

London. Barely larger than a phone box, this diminutive structure is nevertheless quite fancy. Each side displays a carved coat of arms within a ziggurat gable, the door has a Gothic arch, and tiny octagonal railings crown the roof. It was built in 1860 to shelter the ostler, a sort of valet who looked after the horses of those attending Lincoln's Inn. By the end of the century the motorcar had arrived, and the job did not survive long; perhaps the hut is now used by the gardeners or to lock up disruptive young lawyers. Entrance to the Inns is via the sixteenth-century gatehouse facing Lincoln's Inn Fields. In this large square you can also find the house of the architect Sir John Soane, now a free museum crammed with his collections from antiquity. To find the ostler's hut, walk straight ahead past the Great Hall then turn left.

CHERRY TREE
Ye Olde Mitre, 1 Ely Place, EC1N 6SJ

Should you ever find yourself pursued by the Metropolitan Police, you can always buy a few hours by slipping through the iron gates of Ely Place, off Holborn Circus, and claiming sanctuary. This cul-de-sac does not, technically, belong to London but to Cambridgeshire, and the police are forbidden to enter without prior invitation by the Commissioners of Ely Place. The Bishops of Ely kept their townhouse here; wishing to conduct business in London without leaving their diocese, they made the area an exclave. While you wait for the Cambridgeshire Constabulary to make the long drive down the A10, there is plenty to divert you. Ely Place boasts its own chapel (St Etheldreda's, an atmospheric thirteenth-century church) and a pub. Ye Olde Mitre is an intimate, wood-panelled bar with three snug rooms and an outer yard, whose current incarnation dates back to 1772. Behind a glass partition in the pub doorway, the remains of a cherry tree mark the boundary between the bishops' property and that of Elizabeth I's favourite, Christopher Hatton. Legend has it that she and Hatton danced the maypole around this tree. Ye Olde Mitre is accessed via a blink-and-you-miss-it passageway on Hatton Garden, a convenient location for jewel thieves.

ST PAUL'S

THOMAS BECKET
St Paul's Churchyard, EC4M 8AD

The four knights caught up with the Archbishop of Canterbury on his way to vespers, climbing the stairs to the cathedral choir. An eyewitness wrote that when the fourth blow was struck, 'the blood white with the brain, and the brain red with the blood, dyed the floor of the cathedral'. It was 29 December 1170, one month after Thomas Becket had excommunicated Henry II for crowning his son as heir apparent in the archbishop's absence. The ascetic clergyman had spent his tenure clashing with his former friend, and had only recently returned to England after six years in exile. Becket was canonized after his murder, and the shrine holding his remains attracted many visitors to Canterbury until Henry VIII had it destroyed. In the gardens south of St Paul's Cathedral you can find a modern interpretation of Becket's stricken final moments in the form of a 1970 sculpture by Edward Bainbridge Copnall. Resin imitating bronze, the statue is rather expressionist. Becket lies prostrate as if pushed over, his head tilted back with hands aloft for protection or mercy. Becket being a native of Cheapside, the City of London purchased the sculpture and brought him back home.

SHEPHERD AND SHEEP
Paternoster Square, EC4M 7DX

Step through Temple Bar to find yourself in a very twenty-first-century space: the semi-public piazza. The Luftwaffe levelled the lively Paternoster area north of St Paul's and the medieval street plan was replaced by a dreary cluster of cafés and office blocks. New plans were shunted back and forth until 2003, when the area was rebuilt and the Stock Exchange moved in. Its stone and brick materials are a nod to Christopher Wren, but the rather blank buildings are closer to the rationalist style of Mussolini's EUR district in Rome. Despite its tasteful design, the square strikes an inauthentic note. In the wake of the financial crisis, the High Court prevented the Occupy protesters from entering Paternoster Square, decreeing that this 'public space' was private property with no right of way. Two focal points attempt to humanize the space: a gold-crowned column in the style of Wren's Monument stands at less than half the height of the original, as if genuflecting before St Paul's, while a sculpture by Elisabeth Frink is one of the few features to have survived the redevelopment. One of Britain's major post-war artists, Frink was known for her angular, menacing birds, but this is a benign work in which a shepherd clutches his staff and drives five sheep into the square. Apart from the obvious religious connotations, *Shepherd and Sheep* is a nod towards Paternoster's history as a livestock market. The Occupy movement might well look upon it and counsel us to 'Wake up, sheeple.'

PANYER BOY
Panyer Alley, EC2V 6AA

Beside the main entrance to St Paul's station is a row of new cafés and restaurants that make up the edge of the Paternoster Square development. Attached discreetly to the wall is something much older. Within a simple frame is a small engraving of a boy, his face entirely eroded, climbing into what looks like a basket. The panyer boy has been around for so long that nobody knows where he came from or what exactly he is up to. From the late sixteenth century we have written references to an image of a baker's boy sitting on his bread basket, which could be the panyer boy. Some commentators see a woolsack or a coil of rope, Bacchus pressing grapes or the Greco-Roman trope of a boy pulling a thorn from his foot. Evidence points to the boy being older than the accompanying slab of text beneath him: 'When yv have sovght the citty rovnd yet still ths is the highst grovnd avgvst the 27 1688.' We can be grateful that no one has taken the text literally and decided to rehouse the panyer boy at the top of the Shard.

GOLDEN BOY OF PYE CORNER
1 Giltspur Street, EC1A 9DD

He stands stark naked but coated in gold, with corkscrew curls and a sneer on his fat little face. Perching high above us with folded arms, his disdainful gaze is fixed higher still on the heavens, like Nero crossed with the Manneken Pis from Brussels. This indolent homunculus marks the spot where the Great Fire of London was finally stopped. The fire having started at Pudding Lane, contemporary preachers detected a message from an evidently literal-minded God that London had been punished for 'the sin of Gluttony'. The golden boy was initially assigned to the Fortune of War pub, later infamous as a haunt of bodysnatchers, and remained *in situ* when the pub was demolished in 1910.

An inscription on the new building explains that 'the boy was made prodigiously fat to enforce the moral', but in these high-fructose times he could pass for any average inner-city child queueing up for chicken and chips. Pye Corner is at the meeting of Giltspur St and Cock Lane; the latter earned its name as a venue for cockfighting or prostitution, depending on whose story you believe.

MEMORIAL TO HEROIC SELF-SACRIFICE
Postman's Park, EC1A 4EU

Stories of self-sacrifice have an enduring popularity; it's comforting to think that should we find ourselves in peril, other people would be altruistic enough to risk everything for our safety. This tranquil spot, a park created in 1880 on the site of three former churchyards, takes its name from the then-adjacent General Post Office. Visitors do not contemplate Nelson or Wellington, but displays of bravery from ordinary citizens at the Memorial to Heroic Self-Sacrifice. An idea of the painter George Frederic Watts, it is a wall of ceramic tiles, each dedicated to someone who died trying to save others in episodes of fire, drowning or stampeding animals. The youngest was nine years old. Some quote the last words of the dying, some describe bizarre scenarios; one man 'saved a lunatic woman from suicide at Woolwich Arsenal but was himself run over by the train'. The display walks a tightrope between heart-rending and kitsch, but what amplifies its poignancy is that the memorial was never finished. Four of the 120 spaces were filled by tiles upon its opening in 1900. After Watts's death people gradually lost interest in the project. To this day only fifty-four spaces have been taken. After a seventy-eight-year interval, a new tile was added in 2009.

POLICE TELEPHONE POST
1 St Martin's le-Grand, EC1A 4EU

This post, directly beside the entrance to Postman's Park, is just one of a few police posts in central London. Painted a smart and vivid cyan blue, they are topped by a round, coloured lightbulb within a square frame. A sign will usually explain that they are no longer operational. In the period after telephones but before walkie-talkies, these phone posts allowed officers to spend more time on patrol, and the public to contact the nearest station in the event of emergencies. Most of the posts simply contained a phone and a first-aid box, but there were also larger boxes with lighting, heating and a desk inside. It was these boxes that in 1963 were immortalized by the Tardis of *Doctor Who*. By the late sixties the posts and boxes had become obsolete and most were demolished, but a few remain in place. Others can be found at Guildhall Yard,

Walbrook, Old Broad St and Victoria Embankment. As the classic London phone-box design was inspired by the tomb of Sir John Soane, so the lightbulb over police posts is said to take after his lantern design for Dulwich Picture Gallery.

BANK

ALTAR
St Stephen Walbrook, 39 Walbrook, EC4N 8BN

The City churches will forever be associated with their mastermind, Christopher Wren; St Paul's is the iconic masterpiece, with a dome as famous as those of Florence or Rome, but a personal favourite is the dazzling bright white of St Stephen Walbrook. Wren's design is celestial but what makes the church unique is its 1987 rearrangement, when a new altar by sculptor Henry Moore was placed at the centre. Here, modernism is welcomed inside by the Renaissance; the result is not a clash but a perfect synthesis. The altar is made of Travertine marble from the same quarry used by Michelangelo. In this context, the solid block with Moore's characteristic bumps and contours looks timeless and could perhaps pass for an altar from an early Christian catacomb. Protests over its validity as an altar saw the Court of Ecclesiastical Causes Reserved, the highest court in the Anglican Church, meet for only the second time in its history; the altar was given the stamp of approval.

THE CORNHILL DEVILS
54–55 Cornhill, EC3V 3PD

The devil is in the detail, literally so in the case of 54–55 Cornhill. Clad in placid pink terracotta, this late Victorian building sits next door to the Wren church of St Peter's, and at first glance appears an unlikely repository for an immortalized vendetta. The architect was dragged into a territorial dispute with the rector over one foot of contested land, and compelled to redraw his plans. His revenge took the form of three demonic beasts, erected in 1893, who crouch on tiny perches on the façade, staring down at the doorway of St Peter's. With horns on their heads and stegosaurus plates on their backs, the contorted bodies lean forward to spit and hiss curses at churchgoers. One demon is much smaller than the other two, and another is made more monstrous by a plump pair of breasts, provoking blasphemous inklings that they could be an infernal inversion of the Holy Family; the third is thought to be a likeness of the obstinate clergyman in question.

TIVOLI CORNER
The Bank of England, Threadneedle Street, EC2R 8AH

Little of Sir John Soane's famed Bank of England building is left to us except its outer walls; Herbert Baker's expansion of the bank in the twenties and thirties entailed the controversial demolition of most of Soane's work. One partial survivor, at the rear on the corner of Princes St and Lothbury, is Tivoli Corner. Soane was much enamoured of antiquity and a favourite building was the Temple of Vesta at Tivoli, which perches dramatically on a precipice above a deep valley. It inspired this ring of Corinthian columns that add a flourish to the Bank's walls. Baker replaced the crowning attic with a copper dome, topped by a cupola and a golden statue of Ariel. He also opened up the corner with a pair of archways, creating a tunnel to offer pedestrians shelter or a quick shortcut. To pass through is to momentarily find yourself within a Roman mausoleum. Stand out on the street, and the Pantheon-style open oculus in the roof looks onto that golden statue; both intensify the blue of the sky, and provide a wonderful frame for the clouds racing by. In the eyes of Soane's admirers, Baker added insult to injury by recycling two capitals from Tivoli Corner as bird baths at his country house in Cobham. A few paces down Lothbury, a niche houses a statue of Soane, clutching draughtsman's tools and sporting a formidable frown, as well he might. Some suggest that this allusion to a Roman ruin was intended as a gentle reminder to the forces of Capital that all empires eventually fall; we're still waiting.

GRASSHOPPER
Royal Exchange Buildings, EC3V 3NL

Set slightly back from the junction at Bank station, at the rear of the piazza-cum-traffic island, is the dramatic sight of the Royal Exchange. It opened on this site in 1570, but burned down twice and what we see today is Victorian. Its monolithic façade echoes Rome's Pantheon, columns propping up a pediment in which Commerce stands on a plinth, presiding over the transactions of exotic-looking traders from the far-flung corners of the globe. Few notice the large golden insect above the rear steeple, acting as a weathervane. Does it allude to the cautionary fable of the grasshopper and the ant? The mundane truth is that it comes from a family coat of arms. Sir Thomas Gresham was a financial wizard whose ability to play the markets made him indispensable to successive British monarchs. He founded the Exchange as a venue for traders, in imitation of the Bourse at Antwerp. To maximize his profits, Gresham shrewdly added two upper tiers that were rented out to shopkeepers, creating the first shopping mall. It seems fitting that today's Exchange building should be largely given over to luxury boutiques. A few doors along, you can see another Gresham grasshopper, above the entrance to 68 Lombard St.

THE ROYAL PROCESSIONS
1 Poultry, EC2R 8EJ

Within the huddle of prominent buildings around Bank station, the joker in the pack is No. 1 Poultry. It strides into a meeting of sober neo-classical porticoes like a circus clown at a funeral. Often referred to as a keystone of postmodern architecture, after a protracted gestation this controversial building was completed in 1997. The bands of pink and yellow limestone across each wavy segment give it a contemporary look; it's a very hungry caterpillar taking a huge bite out of the City. *Time Out* readers voted it among the five worst buildings in London, but it is only recently that the 'concrete monstrosities' of the 1960s have been reappraised, so later generations may find value in the building's bold insouciance. The 'Royal Processions' frieze of its predecessor from 1875 was saved, and is now incorporated into Poultry's north side. Depicted in terracotta are four monarchs (Edward IV, Elizabeth I, Charles II and Victoria) believed to have passed this spot while entering London. The work is full of detail, personality and humour; to compare the period costumes is like taking in all four series of *Blackadder* at a glance. Courtiers, soldiers and horsemen bark instructions and gesticulate to one another as they clear the way. Charles has two spaniels at his feet. The two queens are carried in a litter and a carriage respectively, and, for once, Queen Victoria looks amused.

CEILING
St Mary Aldermary, Watling Street, EC4M 9BW

A Gothic Wren, this church is something of a rarity: the widow paying for its rebuilding stipulated that Christopher should provide an imitation of the burnt original. St Mary Aldermary's distinctive tower is prominent in the streetscape east of St Paul's, its top parapet bolstered by four slim turrets tapering off into gold caps. The best feature, though, is found inside; a beautiful fan-vaulted ceiling in crisp, icing-sugar white. The fan shapes resemble rows of displaying peacocks, and the gaps in between are filled with shallow domes. The central aisle of the nave, higher than the others, has six white domes with a seventh above the altar that is all red, black and gold heraldry. Admittedly, not everyone will get excited by a church roof, but this ceiling is an all-singing, all-dancing cabaret revue among dour kitchen-sink dramas. Within office hours, the church doubles as a café. In the pews, the congregation slurps on soup and coffee, and the place gets much more use than it would as a place of worship.

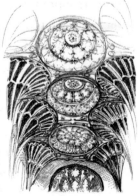

33

LIVERPOOL STREET

TURKISH BATHS
8 Bishopsgate Churchyard, EC2M 1RX

Enter Bishopsgate Churchyard, one of the more pleasing green spaces in the City, and carry on past St Botolph's Church and the abstract sculptures installed between benches. You will find a narrow courtyard before Old Broad St, and at its centre a small kiosk fitted out like the garden shed of an Ottoman sultan. Tiling in bands of cream and red at the base gives way to diverse shades of blue. Its three-sided front has small star windows and longer ones with ogee arches. The windows are bordered by elaborate decorative patterns in terracotta. On the roof is an onion dome in coloured glass, from which protrudes a star and a crescent, and there is more fancy tiling downstairs. This singular little place originally served as an entrance to subterranean Turkish baths; one of five run by the Nevill brothers, this branch was given its arabesque makeover in 1895. The baths closed in the years of post-war austerity but the building periodically springs to life as a cocktail bar or a pizzeria. On my last visit, though, the only sign of life was a letter in the window advising that the leaseholder could collect his belongings from the bailiff.

BEDOUIN TENT
St Ethelburga Centre, 78 Bishopsgate, EC2N 4AG

This tiny church is the calm at the centre of the Bishopsgate storm. With the Gherkin looming over it, St Ethelburga seems the size of a postage stamp, clinging to its spot between the imperial grandstanding of Hasilwood House and a vast empty plot for a proposed skyscraper. The church is first mentioned in 1250, with the familiar structure dating to 1411; its façade was then hidden for centuries behind two shop units. Having survived the Great Fire, St Ethelburga had to be reconstructed from rubble after an IRA bomb in 1993. Turning the other cheek, the church reopened as a peace and reconciliation centre. It is mildly startling to approach the church's rear entrance and discover a small courtyard occupied by a large polygonal tent. Made in Saudi Arabia, the tent was officially opened by Prince Charles. Brown and white goatskin covers its sixteen sides, and the seven windows hold stained glass; the design deliberately excludes religious symbolism and is based on 'sacred geometry'. The effect is somewhere between a gazebo, a nomadic dwelling on the steppes and a wedding reception marquee. As a venue for inter-faith dialogue its purpose is to provide a neutral and unfamiliar space that will open people's minds, man. This sounds nauseating to me, but I come from Belfast, where it is hard not to be cynical about the Conflict Resolution industry.

BETHNAL GREEN

E. PELLICCI
332 Bethnal Green Road, E2 0AG

The rise of coffee chains has largely eradicated their forefathers, the Formica cafés established by Italian families in the 1950s. In recent years, cherished institutions of the West End such as Lorelei and the New Piccadilly Café have been banished to memory. Further east, one classic café has been saved by the bestowal of Grade II listing; this is E. Pellicci on Bethnal Green Rd, still run by the family that opened it several generations ago. The café has been here since 1900 and was a meeting place for the Kray twins. Its façade consists of panels of custard-yellow Vitrolite. Inside, seven small tables are packed into a low-ceilinged room whose walls are panelled with beautiful marquetry: rising suns around the counter and art-deco fan shapes elsewhere. Sensitive modern additions include a Pellicci logo in stained glass on the kitchen door. These cafés introduced post-war Britain to a continental influence and a strong design aesthetic. Many credit them with lifting the country out of drab austerity by providing a breeding ground for youth culture and the swinging sixties. It would be a great loss not to preserve the handful that are left.

MILE END

NOVO CEMETERY
Queen Mary College, E1 4NS

The middle of a busy university campus is an odd place to find a Jewish cemetery. The flat rectangle of land, maybe half the size of a football pitch, does not look particularly pleased about the industrial-looking building whose curved steel frame looms over it. The Novo (new) cemetery has served Sephardic Jews of Spanish and Portuguese origin since 1733; they arrived after Cromwell scrapped a centuries-old law forbidding Jews to live in England. By 1936 the cemetery was filled to capacity, and the expanding Queen Mary campus began to encroach on its grounds. Three quarters of the graves were moved to Essex, at which point the university realized that they were ripping up history and decided to preserve what was left. Today, the cemetery is a peaceful spot. Its perimeter is marked by rust-metal sheets, the name and date of the site cut into them with a stencil font that recalls the street signs of Venice, site of the first Jewish ghetto. The long gravestones lie horizontal, death literally acting as the great leveller. Poking up through the gravel are several thousand Spanish bluebells, whose soft colours compensate for the surroundings.

LEYTONSTONE

HITCHCOCK MOSAICS
Leytonstone Station, Church Lane, E11 1HE

A prophet has no honour in his own country: on the continent, Alfred Hitchcock is regarded as a classic auteur who commanded the studio system to serve his disquieting studies in obsession and madness; on these shores he is slightly misunderstood as a maker of jaunty whodunnits. In 2001, his old manor of Leytonstone attempted to redress this by installing seventeen mosaics in the exit to the Tube station. The shower from *Psycho*, the bell tower from *Vertigo*, Cary Grant fleeing a crop-dusting plane or sneaking across a Riviera rooftop – all your old favourites are there. It may not be high art but it's fun trying to identify each scene, and honouring Hitchcock over E11's other favourite son, David Beckham, is to be applauded. The mosaics are in an Imperial Roman style; the effect is dissonant, but gives them a blast of primitive energy. Assailed by crows, the blonde locks of Tippi Hedren become those of a shrieking Medusa.

Northern Line

North to south, this line serves vast swathes of London and requires ninety-one active trains in rush hour. The branches meet in Zone 2, then split again at Euston – one serving the City, one the West End – only to reunite at Kennington. This is a legacy of the Northern line's origins as an amalgamation of two lines, the City and South London Railway and the Charing Cross, Euston and Hampstead Railway. From Kennington, the line burrows into south London until the suburb of Morden. People travelling from the City to the West End can change at Bank or Waterloo for the two-station Waterloo & City line, a curio that can be travelled from end to end in under four minutes. In 2003, a study into the air quality of the Underground announced that a twenty-minute journey on the Northern line did damage equivalent to one cigarette. Hampstead is the deepest point in the Underground, and

Angel boasts its longest escalator at sixty metres. If the enormous width of the platform at Angel appears odd, this is because it used to be an island platform between tracks running in two directions, one of which has been covered over; you can see this system still in operation at Clapham North and Clapham Common. It is touching to learn that the male voice which booms 'Mind the gap' at Embankment's curved platforms was reinstated at the request of the speaker's widow, who wanted to hear his voice again.

HIGHGATE

HOLLY VILLAGE COTTAGES
Swains Lane, N6 6QJ

Angela Burdett-Coutts was a major philanthropist of the Victorian era and gave away over £3 million. From Nigeria to Jerusalem, she put her wealth to work across the empire, and in London sponsored early experiments in social housing. Holly Village is one of her smaller projects, but what it lacks in scale it compensates for in personality. This mini-estate of eight cottages is a bit of a folly, but by sheer force of will it injects life into its fantasy. To pass through the Gothic archway between the two gatehouses is akin to the magical moment when a

G. K. Chesterton novel departs from reality. The roads from Hampstead to Highgate seem a world away among the dwellings, all turned in to face tiny communal lawns with sundials and picnic tables. These gingerbread houses are thick with concentrated detail. Sharp Gothic spires, stumpy turrets, decorative brick patterns and polygonal gable roofs abound. Although the estate is private, one can still peep over the hedges or enjoy the front houses from Swains Lane, where arcane lettering on the main arch marks the village's construction in 1865. Statues of Burdett-Coutts and her governess/companion Hannah Brown stand either side of the arch. You would need to get on with the neighbours if you lived here, but good surroundings make good neighbours.

LIZZIE SIDDAL'S GRAVE
Highgate Cemetery, N6 6PJ

Highgate Cemetery is as much of a who's who for star-spotters as Père Lachaise cemetery in Paris. Some of the most famous names of the Victorian age, such as Karl Marx and George Eliot, were laid to rest here; more recent arrivals include punk-impresario Malcolm McLaren and the poisoned spy Alexander Litvinenko, buried in an airtight lead coffin to prevent radioactive leaks. One of the macabre stories within these gates is that of Lizzie Siddal. Wife to Dante Gabriel Rossetti and muse of the Pre-Raphaelites, she made an elegant model for such famous paintings as Millais's *Ophelia*. Siddal succumbed to illness, depression and a laudanum addiction, and died of an overdose at thirty-two. A grieving Rossetti enclosed in the coffin his only copy of the love poems he had written for her. Seven years later, Rossetti was an alcoholic himself, struggling to paint or write. His literary agent persuaded him to retrieve the poems; in a twist worthy of Luis Buñuel, witnesses reported that Lizzie's corpse was perfectly preserved and her celebrated red hair had continued to grow after death, filling the coffin with copper locks. Some attribute this to the laudanum, some to an unscrupulous agent hoping to drum up publicity for the poems. The Rossetti family is also located in the cemetery but the man himself rests in Birchington, Kent.

HAMPSTEAD

SHAM BRIDGE
Thousand Pound Pond, Kenwood House, Hampstead Lane, NW3 7JR

Head into the centre of Hampstead Heath and you could be in deepest countryside. It is very easy to lose your bearings within the vast expanse of the Heath, and stumbling into the secluded valley that contains Kenwood House is a delight. Built in the seventeenth-century and remodelled by Robert

Adam, it is home to a wonderful collection of paintings, with Vermeer, Rembrandt, Turner and Gainsborough all making an appearance. Nearby is Thousand Pound Pond, spanned by a white bridge with three low arches and a balustrade railing. This is a clever trick; in fact there is no bridge, just a flat timber façade running along the far bank of the pond. Reflected in the water, the bridge's presence suggests that the pond continues into the woodland beyond, and most visitors are fooled. This is garden landscaping as a stage set. Not everyone was an admirer; the eminent designer Humphry Repton urged its removal, considering it 'beneath the dignity of Kenwood'. A thousand pounds would probably be the nightly fee to rent a house around here, but it is thought likely that the pond earned its name in the twenties when, with property developers circling like vultures, Lord Mansfield sold the land to a conservationist group at £1,000 per acre.

KENTISH TOWN

ST PANCRAS PUBLIC BATHS
18 Prince of Wales Road, NW5 3AW

The Victorians may have been thinking of the sacred springs at Roman Bath when they began building public bath and wash houses. With the Industrial Revolution, the populations of cities doubled within a few decades and the poor were soon living a precarious existence in crowded, unsanitary conditions. The programme worked: adult mortality rates declined as a result. St Pancras bath house, actually in Kentish Town, lured punters in by draping its façade with fantasia. A conical turret and a cupola topped by a spiked Prussian helmet bookend the roof, with high gables in between. The doorways are watched over by writhing gargoyles, as classical figures lounge in the spandrels of the arch. Elsewhere, St George pins down his dragon and St Pancras – beheaded by Diocletian at the age of fourteen – exacts his revenge by standing on a soldier. Best of all is the signage, a sinuous art-nouveau font in gold, demarcating the two doorways as 'Men's First Class' and 'Men's Second Class'. The baths still operate, with a 2010 renovation paid for by converting some of the building into flats.

CAMDEN TOWN

CATS
Carreras Cigarette Factory, Greater London House,
180 Hampstead Road, NW1 7AW

Most north Londoners have but one God, and that God is moggy. In the residential streets of Camden and Islington,

the locals are inveterate cat owners. With most people stuck at work all day, pets need to have an independent streak: this is very much a marriage of convenience. Any visitors from another culture, era or planet could be forgiven for seeing the Carreras Cigarette Factory and assuming it to be a place of cat worship. Just next to Mornington Crescent station, this long white building was designed in 1926 and completed within two years. In the wake of Tutankhamen's tomb being discovered, ancient Egypt had been all the rage. Anything Egyptian was seen as romantic and luxurious, and so this factory was fronted by an Egyptian-style colonnade in bright blue with red and green. Two bronze cats, eight feet tall, stood guard by the entrance and round panels above each column show bust portraits of black cats. With cartoon yellow eyes and pointy whiskers, they seem more Meg and Mog than the goddess Bastet; intentional or not, it makes all this grandeur seem comical. The factory's opening ceremony was pompous: the pavements were covered in sand, actors performing Verdi's *Aida* in the West End gave a performance in costume and there was even a chariot race down Hampstead Rd. In 1959, when Carreras merged with Rothmans and vacated the building, they took the big cats with them. The new occupants decided this Egyptian revival stuff was a naff eyesore and ripped out the lot. By 1996, the tide had turned and architects were summoned to recreate the original twenties design: beware the vagaries of fashion. The restoration omitted the winged sun because of its uncanny similarity to the Nazi eagle.

ANGEL

POLICE GRAFFITI
Myddleton Passage, EC1R 1XQ

It was Juvenal who posed the question, 'Who watches the watchmen?' The question becomes all the more pertinent on Myddelton Passage, a residential street behind Sadler's Wells theatre, when you notice the huge quantity of graffiti carved into a stretch of wall a little past the Shakespeare's Head pub. Etched into these bricks, whose purple and yellow tints make them look bruised, are a bewildering proliferation of numbers and letters. What do they signify, and why did the police allow this criminal act to occur repeatedly? It was said that the marks came from Napoleonic prisoners of war, conscripted to lay bricks in London, but the truth, as revealed by a retired officer, was that police officers themselves were behind the graffiti. The numbers are the officers' collar numbers, followed by the letter indicating their division (in most cases, 'G' for the Finsbury Division based at King's Cross Rd). There is the odd symbol: a crucifix, an anchor, a heart. Sometimes initials and dates are included, which have allowed historians to identify a few of the policemen. The practice began around 1860 and continued until World War I. Its origins remain a mystery. One theory is that the markings were a tribute to an officer who died in action. However, it is more likely that policemen who were posted to stand watch here simply began leaving their mark out of boredom.

OLD STREET

BLAKE, BUNYAN AND DEFOE
Bunhill Fields Burial and Gardens, EC1Y 8ND

Alongside the mock castle barracks of the Honourable Artillery Company on City Rd is Bunhill Fields, a garden containing the remains of a popular cemetery. The 'Bunhill' is derived from Bone Hill, after the bones of

St Paul's old charnel house were deposited here. It was then used as a burial site during the 1665 plague, when the churchyards could not contain the number of dead. The ground was never consecrated, and as such became a popular graveyard for nonconformists. Later, the graves in the northern half were cleared to create parkland and a walkway, while those in the southern half are kept behind railings. Fortunately for celebrity hunters, the memorials of the three most esteemed residents are kept separate in the northern half of the site. John Bunyan is remembered for *Pilgrim's Progress*; his marker is a large chest in smooth stone, topped with a life-size effigy of the author at rest. Daniel Defoe was a prolific pamphleteer, a spy and a sometime civet breeder, whose most enduring work is *Robinson Crusoe*. When his headstone was shattered by lightning, a Victorian children's magazine appealed for donations and spent the funds on a marble obelisk. The third is for William Blake and his wife Catherine. Blake was a maverick artist, poet and visionary, whose verse was set to music for 'Jerusalem', one of England's favourite hymns. His headstone is a 1920s replacement, and stands a few metres from the site of his grave.

MERCURY
Triton Court, 14 Finsbury Square, EC2A 1LQ

Look to the north side of Finsbury Square and, if you squint, you will just about make out a human figure seventy metres up on the top of Triton Court. This tower is an art-deco take on a church steeple, in which straight lines dominate. A four-poster base supports what looks like an empty belfry; rising out of this is an octagonal obelisk with a metal globe on top. Our distant friend, perched perilously on this globe, is a representation of Mercury. With my camera on its strongest setting I can see that he wears a cape and a winged helmet, but with the naked eye he has no more detail than a Subbuteo footballer. One hand clutches a sort of staff, the other is raised as if to keep the sun's glare from his eyes. The front of the ten-storey building includes carvings of Mercury's caduceus symbol, with snakes coiling round a winged rod. Best known as a messenger, Mercury is also the god of commerce and financial gain. As his effigy is almost invisible at street level, perhaps it was not placed at the summit for the benefit of us mere mortals.

BOROUGH

BLUE MEN
Maya House, 134-138 Borough High Street, SE1 1LB

Towards the end of the parade of old pubs, delicatessens, sports bars and estate agents that make up Borough High St is Maya House. A slate-grey thing bereft of any ornament, Maya House would not merit a second glance were it not for the three life-size men scaling its flat surface. Bald and naked, their bodies are a conspicuous Yves Klein blue and each clutches an instrument: a drum and two trumpets. The dour office block makes a good canvas for their antics. The installation looks like it might be an advert for theatre-fillers the Blue Man Group, but is in fact the work of Israeli sculptor Ofra Zimbalista. In her home country, a 'Blue Garden' features nineteen such figures. But what does it all mean? A tribute to the creative spirit and to human endeavour, or a rumination on our vulnerable and futile human condition? Alas, all writings on Zimbalista are in International Art English; for the time being, the trio must remain an enigma.

BLACK CLOCK FACE
St George-the-Martyr, Borough High Street, SE1 1JA

The crossroads at the southern extremity of Borough High St is dominated by the tall spire of St George-the-Martyr.

A church has stood here since Norman times but the current structure went up in the 1730s. The red-brick box of its nave is topped by a Portland stone steeple; St George is an amiable building with classical leanings that conceal a dark side. On three sides of the steeple are a white clock face, illuminated at night. The fourth, facing down Long Lane, has a clock painted black; the reason being, according to legend, that the godless citizens of Bermondsey were the only parishioners who would not contribute towards the building of the church. Spoilsports suggest that the churchmen merely skimped on expenses because this clock face is obscured by the bulk of the nave. Across the road, Little Dorrit Park marks the site of Marshalsea Debtors' Prison, where a young Charles Dickens saw his father incarcerated. This offers a hint as to why the Bermondsey poor might have chosen to conserve what little wealth they possessed.

TOTTENHAM COURT ROAD

GARDENER'S HUT
Soho Square, W1D

A rare green space in the West End, Soho Square is found behind the corner of Oxford St and Charing Cross Rd. The square has been here since the 1670s, and its lawns, trees and benches still make it a popular meeting place and lunch spot for the 'creatives' of Soho. White with warped black timber beams and a sloping roof, the small octagonal hut at the centre of the square might look as old as the adjacent statue of Charles II, and an old rumour suggests that it is connected to Buckingham Palace by tunnel. The prosaic truth is that this mock-Tudor folly was built in 1925 to provide access to an underground electricity substation. The upper storey protrudes slightly and it looks like it would make a good venue for Punch and Judy shows, but the hut currently serves as nothing more than a tool-shed for the Gardens & Parks staff of Westminster Council. A nearby bench commemorates singer Kirsty MacColl of 'Fairytale of New York' fame, who wrote a song called 'Soho Square' and was killed by a motorboat in Mexican waters in 2000.

SELENE
The Nadler Soho Hotel, 10 Carlisle Street, W1D 3BR

Concerned parties have united under the 'Save our Soho' banner; their chief objection is to the replacement of live-music venues, pubs and independent cafés with luxury flats, chain restaurants and boutique hotels. One example of this new Soho, the Nadler hotel, opened in 2013 at the end of a Soho Square side street. Its plain façade is bolstered by a striking statue of *Selene*, the Greek moon goddess. Sculptor Hew Locke has created a work that references art nouveau, Victorian fairy stories, David Bowie's *Ziggy Stardust* and the familiar (for now) sight of Soho drag queens. A black woman with large veined wings stands on a mound of winged masks. Her body and wings are studded with stars, and hundreds more stars sit on arrows protruding from her whole body, making her look like St Sebastian as envisaged by George A. Romero. The piece is evocative of magic and dream, but sharp cactus leaves and arrows give it a sense of danger. The blank masks piled at her feet suggest that the *Queen of Time* from Selfridges has gone Colonel Kurtz and decapitated the subjects of her fairy realm. Locke describes Selene as 'a powerful goddess and magical protector'; Soho had better hope so.

THE SEVEN NOSES OF SOHO
Diverse Locations

The Seven Noses of Soho stand testament to one of the most infamous nights in the history of this licentious quarter of London. One afternoon a group of television executives, celebrating the advent of satellite television, had 3,000 kg of cocaine delivered to the Groucho Club, barricaded the exits and declared that no one would be leaving the premises until the whole lot had been ingested. The denizens of Soho were up to the task, but the overworked hooters of seven partygoers suffered collapse of the septum. Their noses had to be surgically removed and were then scattered around diverse locations to warn future generations that the road of excess leads past the palace of wisdom. I have made up this story on the spot, but there is as much truth to it as there is to the legend that finding all seven noses will guarantee you eternal wealth. Likewise, the story that the nose inside Admiralty Arch dates from the Napoleonic Wars: each time they passed under the arch, Wellington's cavalrymen were said to give it a tweak in mockery of the Corsican general. The noses arrived without explanation or publicity, and it says a lot about the human need for narrative that we were soon concocting myths to rationalize and demystify some plaster noses stuck onto walls. Several tall stories later, in 2011 the cat was let out of the bag when the artist Rick Buckley claimed responsibility. In 1997, he had attached thirty-five casts of his nose to walls in London as a protest against CCTV. The prank, carried out under the nose of a nosy-parker state, was inspired by the Situationists. Most noses were taken down as quickly as they went up but a few have gone the distance and gained repute as a mythic septuplet. There are, at the time of writing, Soho noses on Bateman St, Dean St and Meard St, although the Meard St nose does not look like one of Buckley's group. It is larger and includes some lip and cheek, as if it were a fragment from a classical sculpture. Other noses from the Buckley set do not fall within the boundaries of Soho, but are close by: Great Windmill St, Endell St and that on Admiralty Arch. One further nose loiters outside St Pancras station – but if this counts as part of Soho, then so does Angkor Wat. There is said to be a nose in D'Arblay St, but those who have documented their own searches cannot find it, instead offering the limp suggestion that the skull above a boutique tailor's might count. Even your intrepid author was compelled to admit defeat after ten long minutes of painstaking research. Making a playground of our city streets, the Soho Noses and those who pursue them might well be met with approval at Situationist International HQ. I wish you happy hunting.

NEWMAN PASSAGE
W1T 1EH

It starts with a close-up of an agitated eye. A video camera is stuffed up a sleeve. Through the camera's viewfinder, we see a blonde woman in fur stole and red skirt, pretending to examine shop windows. 'It'll be two quid.' She tilts her head quizzically, trying to work out whether this client will be one of the funny ones. We follow her down a dark passage and up to her room. The skirt comes off. Something makes her stop, and then scream. The camera closes in . . . Michael Powell was one of Britain's best-loved filmmakers, and his wartime classics like *A Matter of Life and Death* and *Colonel Blimp* are celebrations of British tolerance, endurance and good humour. The 1960 film *Peeping Tom* is today regarded as a masterpiece, but at the time it brought Powell's career to an abrupt end. *Psycho* also hit the screens this year, and it's hard to see why the story of a voyeuristic sex murderer caused quite so much moral panic; perhaps because Karl Boehm played him as a sweet, bashful man battling to suppress his worst impulses. The passage where *Peeping Tom* begins is still there, running between Bateman St and Newman St. The Newman St ending is covered and sizzles with atmosphere on a dark night; with cobblestones, bollards, old lamps and railings, it still feels like the film set for a period drama.

Bakerloo Line

Bakerloo, a nickname from a journalist that became officially adopted, is a composite of Baker Street and Waterloo. On its way to Harrow the Bakerloo line covers stretches of north-west London before suburbia: Maida Vale and Warwick Avenue. An unsubstantiated story has Parliament pushing through the necessary legislation for the original Bakerloo line because they wanted a quick route to Lord's Cricket Ground. Charing Cross station has some lovely platform murals by David Gentleman, and Baker Street features the familiar silhouette image of Sherlock Holmes. Its ten platforms are also the most of any Tube station: access to the Metropolitan line platforms is under an elegant arch that advertises the stops in each direction. Keep an eye out for the beautiful twenties 'World Clock' in Piccadilly Circus's entrance hall, a linear clock showing the time zones across a map of the world. The

Bakerloo dips its toes into south London before stopping short at Elephant & Castle, for which we can hardly blame it. An aborted 1940s project to extend the tracks to Camberwell has left sidings just after Elephant & Castle, which hold a pair of trains overnight. The authorities are forever considering the extension of this line to the Old Kent Rd, the last substantial area in inner London yet to be blessed by regeneration, and on to Lewisham, which is suffering its own Renaissance. No one seems to know where the required billions would come from and the 'Bakerlooisham' line looks decades away.

BAKER STREET

MONKEY AND HUNCHBACK
Portman Mansions, Chiltern Street, W1U 6NS

Baker Street is a chaotic station, with a perpetual stream of tourists for Sherlock Holmes's house or Madame Tussaud's. On the opposite side of Marylebone Rd, away from the crowds, is Portman Mansions, a six-floor group of flats from the 1890s gathered around the top of Chiltern St. Between its chimneys are ziggurat gables echoing a Flemish merchant house, and on the top of each sits a little animal: dragons, dogs or gargoyles, which are fairly normal on buildings like this. But on the corner of Chiltern St and Porter St you will encounter somebody with a bit more personality: a cheeky monkey with a mouth as wide as Zippy from *Rainbow*, whose eyes bulge as he stares down at us. Unfortunately one of his feet seems to have dropped off, but the other grasps the perimeter of the roof and we can see his curly tail behind. He has a counterpart further down Porter St in the form of a robed and tonsured Quasimodo, who grips the parapet for dear life and gurns as if he were suffering a vertiginous panic attack. This pair are not present in the architect's plans and are said to have appeared overnight in 1935. Whatever their provenance, they are a humane touch that adds a splash of colour to some otherwise taciturn dwellings.

GOLDEN GIRLS

St Marylebone Parish Church, 17 Marylebone Road, NW1 5LT

Completed in 1817, this is the fourth incarnation of Marylebone's parish church. There is a particularly fine view of it from Regent's Park, where it provides a full stop for the classical Nash terraces of York Gate. This was Dickens's local church for twelve years, and Robert Browning and Elizabeth Barrett married here in secret before eloping to Italy. Byron was christened at its predecessor and Lord Nelson was a regular. It has many features of a classical English church – a box shape, pews and perimeter galleries – which give way to a flight of fancy around the recessed semi-dome apse, added in 1884. This is dominated by Edward Armitage's Pre-Raphaelite frescoes, where angels pluck on harps and guitars. The exterior looks fairly conventional until you look up and find your eyes dazzled by eight golden, female angels, propping up the small dome that caps the spire. Paired to represent the four winds, these smiling caryatids have a Botticellian beauty. One arm dangles idle, and the pose is so casual that they could just as easily be stretching out mid-yawn. Each one extends a coquettish bare leg through her robes. The caryatids that the artist J. C. F. Rossi provided for St Pancras New Church are more famous, but these ones look like they know how to have a good time.

OXFORD CIRCUS

PROSPERO AND ARIEL
Broadcasting House, Portland Place, W1A 1AA

One of the most famous works by Eric Gill, one of the most eminent sculptors of the twentieth century, is a relief of *Prospero and Ariel* for the BBC's Broadcasting House at Langham Place. The BBC no doubt saw themselves as the omnipotent Prospero, and the airwaves as the magical sprite at their service. Gill, however, aimed to depict the pair as two-thirds of the Trinity. Holding his flute, a smiling Ariel raises up his arms and looks ready for take-off. Prospero cradles the boy between his arms and legs – in our guarded, suspicious times, the image of an old man looming over a naked boy is an immediate reminder of recent scandals at the BBC. Furthermore, Eric Gill's work has taken on a highly controversial sheen since a 1989 biography revealed that the artist was sexually active with his own children, his sister and his dog. Now and again people call for his carvings to be pulled down. It is certainly not what they had in mind when commissioning Gill, but an argument could be put forth that having his work adorn the BBC acts as a wholly appropriate badge of shame and a warning against the abuses of power; likewise, his Stations of the Cross that adorn Westminster Cathedral. Mile End's Queen Mary College has some excellent Gill reliefs that depict such disciplines as drama, music, boxing, and another epicene boy blowing on a woodwind instrument.

MUSICAL PUTTI
1 Wigmore Street, W1U 1AD

With an underground car park at one end and some glorious townhouses at the other, Cavendish Square is something of a frontier between the chaos of Oxford Circus and the salubrious addresses to its north. On the side of one such house, at the corner of Wigmore St and

Harley St, is a sight that surely would raise a smile from the most exasperated of shoppers. Beside a front door is a long frieze depicting an eleven-piece putti orchestra. One bashes out chords on a piano, others saw away at string instruments, and the last cherub struggles to master an outsize drum. What looks like stucco is actually painted concrete, and two ladies in togas stand either side of the door. The sculptor was Gilbert Bayes. The frieze looks like it might advertise the wares at nearby Wigmore Hall; in fact, the building was a showroom for Brinsmead pianos. A lesson in globalization: Brinsmead was taken over by Cramer & Co., itself taken over by Kemble & Co. Yamaha bought the latter and in 2009 closed the doors on Britain's last piano manufacturer.

CRAIGLEITH STONE
Chandos House, 2 Queen Anne Street, W1G 9LQ

Sitting quietly in a corner of Chandos St and Queen Anne St, Chandos House, a three-storey Georgian building, has very little adornment compared with its neighbours. Yet something about it immediately catches the eye. The stone is grey, sandy and gritty; it makes the townhouse look as if it hailed from a northern city and had just stepped off a train at King's Cross. It is no surprise to learn that it was built by Robert Adam, the neo-classical architect who had such a hand in the creation of Edinburgh's New Town. He clad Chandos House in Craigleith stone to showcase the quarry that was creating a masterpiece in the heart of Midlothian. This unofficial Scottish embassy became the Austro-Hungarian embassy in the nineteenth century and for a quarter-century was home to Prince Esterhazy, grandson to Haydn's patron of the same name. A spectacularly wealthy Hungarian nobleman straight out of a Stefan Zweig novel, the prince used Chandos House to stage lavish parties and banquets and was seldom out of the gossip columns. Today, the Royal Society of Medicine maintains this tradition by chiefly hiring out the house as a wedding venue.

FLAMES
Palladium House, 1–4 Argyll Street, W1F 7TA

Palladium House (formerly Ideal House) is to be found on the corner of Argyll St and Great Marlborough St. Seconds from Oxford Circus station, hordes of pedestrian traffic pass by without seeing, it as it is sandwiched between the London Palladium and the mock-Tudor frontage of Liberty. The walls are clad in lustrous black granite, but the passer-by has to crane their neck to view its most handsome feature: a decorative enamel cornice around the top floor. It is art deco with a typical Egyptian twist. Tongues of gold appear to drip down the walls, flecked at their centre with reds, blues and greens. The tall multistorey features just this one embellishment, like a single piece of jewellery matched with a little black

dress. Today its showrooms host chain restaurants, but the doorways have some pleasing modernist motifs. The cornice is suggestive of fire, and Ideal House was indeed built for the National Radiator Company. It is the only European building of Raymond Hood, designer of the Rockefeller Centre and believed to be the inspiration for Peter Keating, Ayn Rand's 'second-hander' nemesis in *The Fountainhead*. Nikolaus Pevsner instructed his reader to stand between Ideal House and Liberty, and 'stop and consider which of two evils of our present civilization he may be readier to put up with'.

PICCADILLY CIRCUS

FRUIT AND FLOWERS
St James's Church, 197 Piccadilly, W1J 9LL

The master carver Grinling Gibbons is often dubbed 'the Michelangelo of wood', and this Piccadilly church contains some of his most virtuoso work. His decorative garlands have an agile quality and are lifelike to an enthralling degree. Born in 1648 and raised in Rotterdam, he moved to England and was discovered by John Evelyn while renting a cottage on his Deptford estate. Commissions from Charles II and future kings kept him busy. This altarpiece in limewood depicts a wide array of fruits, flowers, vines, seashells, birds and other objects in a symmetrical arrangement. At the centre is the Christian symbol of the pelican piercing her breast to feed her young. The technique is startling. Like an Islamic tile pattern, Gibbons's design helps to fill out an altarpiece for a faith which frowned upon figurative icons. Peapods are a fixture in Gibbons's work, and legend has it that an unopened peapod indicated he had not yet been paid for the job. Also worth seeing here is Gibbons's marble font, in the shape of the tree of knowledge with Adam and Eve standing at its base; William Blake was baptized in it. St James's is one of Wren's larger churches and he named it as his favourite. Today, when very few can afford to live in the parish, it has reinvented itself as a concert venue; a particularly progressive church, it allows the homeless to sleep in one aisle.

STREET LIFE
3 St James's Square, SW1Y 4JU

This distinguished square is lined by some excellent Georgian buildings and some decidedly undistinguished interlopers from the twentieth century. No. 4 was home to Nancy Astor, first woman to take a seat in Parliament. Next door, No. 3 is a neo-Georgian effort built in 1933. We need not linger long on the structure itself but the first floor is lined with delightful friezes depicting scenes from London street life. The bellowing of a costermonger draws attention to his barrel of fruit. Two boys hold out a coin, and their envious sisters fume in silence. A monkey perches on top of an organ grinder's instrument. The musician has raised his hand as if to chastise the animal, but both are staring each other out and the monkey's expression suggests 'Who, me?' or perhaps 'You wouldn't dare, mate'. The attention to minute details makes the carving vivid and human. The scenes are far more evocative of Georgian London than the bland office block's attempt to pass itself off as Queen Anne period. Facing No. 3, against the garden railings, is a memorial to the policewoman Yvonne Fletcher, installed at the suggestion of film director Michael Winner. In 1984 a major diplomatic crisis occurred when, during a student protest, Fletcher was killed by a gunshot from within the Libyan embassy. Incidents such as this and the Lockerbie bombing no doubt made Britain eager to assist in the downfall of Colonel Gaddafi, although what has replaced him appears to be far worse.

22 EMINENT MEN
6 Burlington Gardens, W1J OPE

Visitors to the blockbuster exhibitions of the Royal Academy enter its courtyard from Piccadilly. Only when one notices the northern façade, on Burlington Gardens, does it feel as if they are all using the tradesman's entrance. Thirteen bays in Italianate style are surrounded by symmetrical statues, pillars, pilasters and balconies. A pair of stumpy clock towers look as if they long to be campaniles when they grow up. Why should the rear of the Royal Academy be so elaborate? The reason is that this has always been a separate building, backing on to the gallery at Burlington House. The RA acquired it in 1997, since when a number of attempts to integrate the pair have failed to get off the ground. 6 Burlington Gardens was built for London University. It is the sooty statues that catch the eye; twelve stand on the roof, six in niches on the wings and four above the central portico. The effect is very like standing before one of Palladio's palaces in Vicenza: two's company, twenty-two's a crowd. The statues represent science, law, art and medicine, with the net cast wide to include Newton, Bentham and Milton along with favoured ancients and foreigners such as Archimedes, Cicero, Galileo and Goethe. The inclusion of Justinian among the six ancients raises an eyebrow. The long-suffering architect Sir James Pennethorne, on the last job before his death, had to put up with design by committee and alterations being requested even as the building went up, which accounts for the eccentric result. This, and the lack of surrounding space, give it a slightly stilted appearance – but it is the eccentricity that keeps you looking.

THE BEADLES
Burlington Arcade, 51 Piccadilly, W1J 0QJ

This is the only living human entry in this book. At either entrance of the shopping arcade beside the Royal Academy you will spot the beadles: men in the anachronistic garb of top hats, capes and frock coats (useful protection from all that fog). Beadles do not have particularly pleasant connotations – their mention reminds us of Oliver Twist asking for some more – but while Mr Bumble was a sort of Victorian Police Community Support Officer, these beadles appear to be security guards in fancy dress. As you might expect, the backstory is more distinguished. Burlington Arcade's beadles are the oldest and smallest police force in the world, and the first ones were veterans of Waterloo. In 1819 Lord Cavendish had the roofed arcade built to prevent the public from throwing litter and oyster shells over his wall into Burlington House. As Sir Robert Peel was yet to form the Met, Cavendish recruited beadles from his old regiment, the 10th Royal Hussars. The arcade may have been inspired by the glass-topped Passage du Caire in Paris, itself inspired by the souks which Napoleon's forces saw in Egypt. Burlington Arcade is still replete with luxury goods and its beadles continue to enforce a rigid set of rules that prohibits open umbrellas, large parcels, prams, chewing gum, humming, running or whistling (the latter was a popular alarm signal for pimps, prostitutes and pickpockets).

CHARING CROSS

MUTILATED SCULPTURES
Zimbabwe House, 429 Strand, WC2R 0JR

Whether for iconoclasm or censorship, Protestants have always been enthusiastic participants in the mutilation of sculpture. In 1908, Jacob Epstein provided 18 nude reliefs for the new British Medical Association building on the Strand. Portraying ageing folk with authentically drooping appendages, the figures were more Egon Schiele than Titian and the public were shocked by their frankness. In the 1930s, the Rhodesian High Commission moved into the building and hacked off heads, breasts and genitals on the pretext that the public were imperilled, although not in a moral sense: the Portland stone was said to be disintegrating. Look up as you pass, and the unhappy remains of the sculptures seem to be receding into the walls, turning their backs on a reactionary, hostile world. They could be inscrutable fragments from a distant age of enlightenment, like the headless, limbless figures of the Elgin marbles. Rhodesia House is now Zimbabwe House, and a focus for protests against the disreputable governance of Robert Mugabe, which renders the maimed reliefs grimly apt.

REAR WINDOW
St Martin-in-the-Fields, Trafalgar Square, WC2N 4JL

Facing onto Trafalgar Square, where the swagger of its steeple compensates for the reticence of the National Gallery's dome, this is one of the most recognizable churches in London. For its first hundred years, this was not so: built in 1722, the church arrived into a crowded area and the American writer J. P. Malcolm remarked that its façade 'would have a grand effect, if the execrable watch-house and sheds before it were removed'. Today the church has a popular crypt café, and its candlelit evening concerts are a staple for any tourists yet to tire of *The Four Seasons* or *Eine Kleine Nachtmusik*. Commuters who use the church path as a shortcut to Charing Cross station might notice the unusual central window at its

eastern end, which was installed in 2008. A grid of small, clear glass panes within steel framing is interrupted by a lopsided oval pane of glass, and the frames around this central pane are warped, as if it were a stone causing ripples in the water; the distortion runs in four directions, making a discreetly cruciform shape. The oval panel is finer than the dense glass surrounding it, and light pours into the church through this aperture. It is suggestive of the soul or spirit; abstract art to illuminate abstract concepts. The artist is Shirazeh Houshiary, an Iranian woman who has lived in London for many years.

WELLINGTON'S HORSE BLOCK
Athenaeum, 107 Pall Mall, SW1Y 5ER

Just off Pall Mall, Waterloo Place abounds with kings, statesmen and war heroes. One could easily overlook the two long slabs of granite sitting on the kerbstone, one outside the Athenaeum and one on the opposite pavement. These are horse blocks, that helped less robust riders to mount and dismount. A plaque tells us tersely that the Athenaeum block was placed here 'by the desire of the Duke of Wellington, 1830'. This ages Wellington at sixty-one, around the time of two spells as Prime Minister. 1830 was also the year when Napoleon's nemesis was guest of honour at the inaugural Liverpool–Manchester train journey. He remained an implacable opponent of the railways for the rest of his life, having decided that they would 'encourage the lower classes to travel about', an attitude that persists today, as when Conservative minister Oliver Letwin declared that 'We don't want more people from Sheffield flying away on cheap holidays'. The Iron Duke has statues and monuments all over the country, but this chipped and weathered piece of street furniture may speak more eloquently of his place in British life.

NAZI DOG
Carlton House Terrace Gardens, SW1Y 5AG

Underneath the grand old Duke of York and his forty-metre column is a narrow patch of greenery containing a tree, and a corner of a foreign field that is forever the Third Reich. Guides to the quirkier sights of London seldom fail to mention the grave of Giro, the Nazi dog. He could sniff out every partisan hideout within a ten-mile radius and when Stalingrad fell he died with his right paw held aloft, barking 'The Horst Wessel Song' at the top of his voice. The truth has been somewhat distorted here. Carlton House Terrace is a splendid John Nash creation and Nos. 7–9, currently home to the Royal Society, previously served as the German embassy. Giro was owned by Leopold von Hoesch, Weimar Germany's final appointment to the post of ambassador. Hoesch remained in place until his death in 1936, when Ribbentrop replaced him. Well liked by the British, Hoesch's passing was marked by an eighteen-gun salute in Hyde Park. Fascinating video footage shows a coffin draped in the swastika flag, receiving full honours as it is carried through the streets of London. Giro's little gravestone is marked 'ein treuer Begleiter!', or true companion, and is protected by a wooden and Perspex frame. You will find it next to a flight of steps under the Duke of York's column.

WATERLOO

GRAFFITI TUNNEL
LEAKE STREET, SE1 7NN

The French tend to name their termini after battles Napoleon won, the British after battles Napoleon lost. The entrance to Waterloo station is a vast victory arch in memory of the many railway employees killed in World War I, with Britannia presiding over two sculpture groups representing war and peace. We must continue down York Rd to find Waterloo's underbelly, Leake St, which is largely a tunnel that runs underneath the train tracks. When the station was the initial terminus for Eurostar, it was used for pick-ups and drop-offs, and in 2008 the street was pedestrianized when Eurostar migrated to St Pancras. Banksy, that consummate publicist, gave Leake St a high profile by inviting thirty-nine graffiti artists to participate in a punning Cans Festival that saw their work decorate the tunnel walls. Since then it has been a place where graffiti art is tolerated by the authorities, and arguably sanitized. Leake St is a popular location for promotional photo shoots and theatre companies. The tunnel is an exhibition space with guest themes; street graffiti has grown up, and been absorbed by the establishment it set out to confront.

ELEPHANT & CASTLE

FARADAY MEMORIAL
Elephant & Castle Roundabout), SE1 6TG

When Michael Faraday was born in Newington in the late eighteenth century, it was a sleepy hamlet in Surrey. The area has long since been swallowed up by inner London, and the great scientist would struggle to recognize his birthplace were he to see his abstract memorial that now stands within Elephant & Castle roundabout. An autodidact of humble beginnings, Faraday's discovery of the electromagnetic field ushered in the age of electricity. Designed in the brutalist style that was all the rage in 1961, the memorial consists of the casing for the Tube station's electricity substation. It is a large box covered by square metal panels that look like very dense glass. With nothing in the way of explanation, it stands within several lanes of traffic much like the monolith from Stanley Kubrick's *2001*. As a deprived area very close to Waterloo and London Bridge, the Elephant has been marked out for regeneration. The huge Heygate Estate was demolished and its developers promise luxury flats for 'the wealthier breed of pioneering urbanaut'. Faraday's memorial was made a listed structure in 1996 and given coloured 'disco' lighting in 2002, and 'Faraday Island' is expected to remain centre-stage in the gentrified Elephant to come. The shopping centre opposite, surrounded by concrete underpasses, is worth a visit as a prime example of a London that is rapidly vanishing. It is a poor place for poor people that nevertheless puts up a defiant gaudiness.

SOVIET TANK
Mandela Way, SE1 5UX

Del Boy from *Only Fools and Horses* famously claimed that Elephant & Castle got its name when Richard I was besieged by the troops of Hannibal. No doubt he would concoct a similarly fanciful story about the decommissioned tank that sits near the top of the Old Kent Road, in which it is a relic from a repressive government's failed attempt to repress a 'Bermondsey Spring'. The Old Kent Road is at present a dreary area dominated by retail parks, large supermarkets and car parks. Bellicose among the blandness, the tank is quite a jolt. It was placed there by a property developer who bought the derelict, fenced-off patch of weeds and rubble in which it sits. Piqued when he was refused permission to build flats, he asked to install a tank instead; assuming he meant a septic tank, the council acquiesced. The tank is a T-34 model of the type heavily used in World War II, and this particular vehicle served in the Czech army. Having retired from running over students in Prague, it made its way to England for use in the film *Richard III*, which recast the monarch (Ian McKellen) as a fascist leader in 1930s Britain. The tank is frequently painted in fresh colour schemes, ranging from the Vorticist to the hippy-dippy. At the time of writing it is a fetching orange with tiger stripes.

Piccadilly Line

The venerable old Piccadilly line runs generally from south-west to north, catering for old money and new alike. Starting around Heathrow, Hounslow and Brentford, it takes in the exclusive neighbourhoods of Kensington before hurtling into the West End and Bloomsbury, coming out the other end around Islington and continuing through Haringey and Enfield. Twenty-six of its stations were designed by the celebrated architect Charles Holden, who managed to create real beauty from the raw materials of brick, concrete and glass. His stations are simple and highly functional, but their modernist look remains striking; Arnos Grove is perhaps the best loved. There are interesting antique objects dotted around the stations, such as the blue staff-only phone booths on the platforms of South Kensington, with a bell labelled 'Station Inspector'. Some disused features have been covered over; the onerous number of stairs at Holborn are there to cover the platforms to the defunct station at Aldwych, now used only by film crews. Holloway Road station has an experimental spiral escalator, which broke almost immediately and has never been resurrected. During World War II, stretches of the Piccadilly line's tunnels were used as safe storage for the Elgin marbles.

RUSSELL SQUARE

TRAGEDY AND COMEDY
Rada, 64–66 Gower Street, WC1E 6ED

Sandhurst for luvvies. From Gielgud to Gambon, Michael Sheen to Sean Bean, a great many of Britain's most famous actors learned their trade at this institution, established in 1904. The academy is not to everyone's taste; as a teenager from the mean streets of Hackney, Harold Pinter found the place 'full of poofs and ponces'. The playwright dropped out after feigning a breakdown. Above the Gower St doorway is a wry art-deco sculpture from 1927. Two totemic figures stand either side of a slab engraved with the academy's name. The pair hold up large Greek drama masks, the faces side on, that cover their heads. The cheerful young girl poses with a tragic mask that has a sad frown, tears running down its cheeks. The morose man opposite has a grinning comic mask, at odds with his own sourpuss snarl. The comedy/tragedy masks are a staple theatre motif, but this sculpture uses them to make a deceptively simple observation. Moderating our true selves, feelings and opinions to get along and avoid conflict, perhaps we are all actors.

APOLOGY
Brunei Gallery, Thornhaugh Street, WC1H 0XG

In a corner of Russell Square, a row of elegant Georgian townhouses is bookended by a blocky and no-frills modernist building in red brick. The style sets it apart, but its general shape and the spacing of the windows is a deferential allusion to the Georgian, like a diminishing echo as you walk away from the square. This is the Brunei Gallery, part of the SOAS (School of Oriental and African Studies) campus. So far, so unremarkable, until you notice a plaque that reads, 'The University of London hereby records its sincere apologies that the plans of this building were settled without due consultation with the Russell family and their trustees and therefore without their approval of its design.' From Euston to Covent Garden, huge swathes of the land belonged to the Russell family's Bedford Estate. In the nineteenth century, universities were given the right to make compulsory purchase orders, with the proviso that the Russell family be allowed power of veto over new structures facing onto Russell

Square. This was overlooked in the design of the Brunei Gallery, so the wronged estate was allowed to choose the wording of this plaque, which tugs its forelock dutifully and begs forgiveness. Ironically, a second plaque beneath shows that the gallery received the Civic Trust award for sensitive design; but it's the principle of the thing, old boy. The gallery's sponsor is the Sultan of Brunei, who famously paid Michael Jackson $17 million to perform at his fiftieth birthday.

SNOB SCREENS
The Lamb, 94 Lamb's Conduit Street, WC1N 3LZ

Slightly frayed but essentially unspoilt, the Lamb is a homely pub between Russell Square and Theobald's Rd. No music, no fruit machines, no Sky Sports; the pub you will have in your mind's eye while reading a Patrick Hamilton novel will not differ vastly from this one, and it has some literary links. Dickens was a regular, while Ted Hughes and Sylvia Plath met here for dates. Step inside and you face a U-shaped bar area; some interesting pieces of

Victoriana to have been preserved are the 'snob screens' lining either side of the bar. These are panels of glass that rotate on hinges, with a small gap underneath for the exchange of pints and pounds. The idea was to give drinkers greater privacy and anonymity. Behind the screens they could be served without being seen by the bar staff, which came in handy for those who considered themselves Brahmin caste, or just happened to be with a lady who was not their wife. If bartenders suspected that a customer had had enough, or was committing mischief, they could discreetly tilt a panel to check up on them. The glass is frosted with a star pattern etched onto the centre of each panel. In the front windows, above glazed green tiling, the frosted glass depicts lambs and the pub walls are lined with vintage photos. The Lamb takes its name from Lamb's Conduit St, which in turn takes its name, astonishingly, from a man called Lamb having installed a conduit for clean water.

GOLDBUG VARIATIONS
London School of Hygiene & Tropical Medicine,
Keppel Street, WC1E 7HT

Sun Tzu said that to know your enemy, you must become your enemy, a lesson taken to heart by the London School of Hygiene & Tropical Medicine. A number of historic Georgian houses on Keppel St were demolished to make way for this building – Parnell, Trollope and Constable lived here – so it is just as well that it houses one of the world's top research institutions. The college is a twenties take on the classical Portland stone edifice. Under the roof balustrade is a ribbon with the names of great scientists, separated by laurel wreaths: Jenner, Lister and Pasteur are up there. The doorway is dark, streaky marble, embossed with gold lettering. Above it, Apollo and Artemis ride in a horse-drawn chariot, but the most distinctive, and unexpectedly charming, detail is to be found on the metal art-deco balconies. Attached to each end is an insect, painted gold. There are flies, fleas, ticks, mosquitoes and lice (as well as a snake and a rat). No René Lalique brooches, they adhere to simple, factual, from-the-encyclopaedia representations, but they are fine pieces of craftsmanship. These are nasty little beasts that we are instructed to find repellent, but once a threat is neutered, you can find something to admire in the most unlikely places.

HOLBORN

SNUGS
Princess Louise, 208 High Holborn, WC1V 7EP

The sixth child of Victoria and Albert, Princess Louise was something of a cuckoo in the nest. She was a talented painter and sculptor with liberal, feminist views, who felt distaste for the cult of grief initiated by her father's death. The Princess Louise pub named in her honour puts the palace into 'gin palace'. Lamps resemble incense holders and the decorative, multicoloured tiling approaches the heights of Islamic art. Timber and frosted glass divide the space around a horseshoe bar into seven areas including four private little snugs. Nabbing one of these snugs for your friends feels like having a box at the opera. They are your own pew in a great basilica of booze. The partitions were done away with in the mid-twentieth century, but restored a few years ago when Samuel Smith's brewery took over. Even the urinals are listed, and you'll see why if you pop downstairs. The pub was built in 1872 and its interiors date from 1891. Ewan MacColl, communist folk musician and father of Kirsty, ran the influential Ballads and Blues club here in the 1950s.

AFRICAN SCULPTURE GROUP
Africa House, 64–78 Kingsway, WC2B 6AH

Kingsway was intended to be a grand boulevard in the manner of Paris. The architecture tends to sag somewhat in the middle, but at Aldwych and Holborn it boasts some lofty edifices from Britain's distant days as a superpower. Africa House opened in 1922 to trade commodities. A cornice on the seventh of eight floors houses a group of allegorical sculptures, carved by Benjamin Clemens, which represents Britain's colonial interests in the usual paternalistic way. Britannia is enthroned at the centre, with her shield and a cumbersome broadsword. On her right are two robed and bearded Arabs, while a camel, crocodile and an awfully handsome lion look out. On her left sits a young man with a pith helmet, examining his rifle, while a strapping, semi-naked black man carries a heavy load on his back. The sculpture seems to place him with the camel in the 'beasts of burden' category. After these two are a snake, a wildebeest and an elephant slumped on the floor, who I fear has just been felled by the chap with the gun. The neatly categorized hierarchy of this group portrait has all the authenticity of an Um Bongo advert. With the benefit of hindsight we know that the empire would vanish in a few decades, and such grandstanding now seems to have served the purpose of self-reassurance. We are not looking at the continent in all its complexities and contradictions, but a flat caricature of how a docile, servile Africa would have been in a more convenient world. The unlikely menagerie is so high up on the building that the best view is from across the road. Africa House was redeveloped in 2013. The publicity described its location, a few doors from Holborn station, as 'Midtown', overlooking the fact that London has no Uptown or Downtown. Developers have also attempted to reassign Fitzrovia as 'Noho', and the disease is spreading; recent months have seen Lower Holloway Road rechristened 'Loho', and Lewisham 'Newisham'. The Mayor should nip this absurdity in the bud by issuing fines.

SICILIAN AVENUE
WC1A 2QD

Walk north from Holborn station, and on your left a small uncovered arcade will transport you to the sun-kissed Mediterranean. Cool down with a lemon granita, tuck into freshly caught lobster, marvel at the Moorish and Norman architecture and be extremely careful what you say about the Mafia. I exaggerate: Sicilian Avenue's name is a slightly fanciful flourish for what is two short rows of retail units with flats and offices above. Here is a diagonal passage, entered at either end through a row of Ionic columns, topped by a balustrade and carvings of urns. It was built in 1910, when it was still the fashion to embellish buildings. On a summer's evening, when punters are dining *al fresco*, its Edwardian adornments do faintly evoke the baroque style of the Mezzogiorno. The first two floors are stone with classical pilasters, above them red terracotta with swanky oriel windows. Some of the eateries within, whose owners must holiday in very different regions of Italy from me, assert that it resembles 'the prettiest backstreets of an Italian hilltop village'. Sicilian Avenue would probably have more magnetism in a less corporate city than London, which can think of nothing better to do with it than to cram in the usual chain restaurants and shops. If you are on the way to Bloomsbury, as pedestrian cut-throughs go it's still much preferable to a dark alleyway.

COVENT GARDEN

THE EARS OF COVENT GARDEN
Floral Street, WC2E 9HW

As a supplement to the Soho noses, anyone whose tastes run more towards *Blue Velvet* may wish to look for the ears of Floral St, a street heavy with fashion boutiques. There are two ears that I could spot. The man responsible is artist/illustrator Tim Fishlock, and the ears are reportedly casts of his own. People say that more ears can be found scattered across London but nobody seems to know where exactly. The artist has seemingly maintained radio silence regarding his intentions. It could be another oblique comment on state surveillance, an allusion to Van Gogh or David Lynch, or perhaps a literal rendering of the phrase 'walls have ears'. Seen apart from the context of a human head, the ears look strange and perplexing. The idea that someone was secretly listening in on us was a widespread preoccupation during the Cold War. Today, thanks to the internet, citizens volunteer the information themselves.

CHARLES MACKLIN MEMORIAL
St Paul's Church, Bedford Street, WC2E 9ED

From Italianate piazza to red-light district, from green-grocers' distribution market to tourist trap, Covent Garden has a chequered history and Inigo Jones's church has watched over it all. This is where Henry Higgins met Eliza Doolittle; were *Pygmalion* written today, it would consist of a French field-trip student encountering a fire-eating unicyclist. St Paul's was built in 1631 but with its large pediment and four gigantic Tuscan columns, it looks centuries older. It is unusual for a large church to look so bare, but the Reformation was still recent. Devoid of chapels or aisles, the interior is called 'the finest barn in Europe'. At the heart of Theatreland, St Paul's is known as the actors' church and one of the many thespians remembered there is Charles Macklin, a fiery Irishman who revolutionized theatre in the eighteenth century. In a long career that lasted until his nineties, Macklin's most celebrated role was Shylock in *The Merchant of Venice*. Shylock was played comically at the time but his delivery of a darker, more nuanced performance won him immediate fame. Macklin's career was dogged by controversy, most notably in 1735 when he was sentenced for manslaughter. Performing in a farce at the Theatre Royal, Drury Lane, Macklin fought over a wig with another actor, Thomas Hallam, and thrust his cane through Hallam's eye and into his brain, killing him. His simple stone plaque at St Paul's features a short poem and a theatrical mask with a dagger plunged through one eye. It is a vaudeville flourish of questionable taste, but that's actors for you. The plaque is considered a sincere gesture of contrition, rather than a boast.

LEICESTER SQUARE

LITTLE COMPTON STREET
Charing Cross Road, WC2H 0DT

Here is a curio that thousands walk over without realizing. London has acquired several layers of history; many of the Thames's tributary rivers are buried under our roads, and the Victorians built several miles of utility tunnels for gas, water and sewage. The myths surrounding subterranean London are legion, but few know one piece of evidence that hides in plain sight. Opposite Molly Moggs pub, where Old Compton St meets Charing Cross Rd, a small traffic island sits in the middle of the road. Peer through the grating and you will get some odd looks from the passing crowds, but you will also find a street beneath the street. On the subterranean wall, two street signs, dark blue above white, name the location as Little Compton St, a Victorian road that has vanished from the *London A–Z*. Some commentators suggest the grille looks down on the original street, but it scarcely seems plausible that the nineteenth-century street level could be this far below. More likely, the signs indicate the location for engineers working in the utility tunnels, or they could date from a much earlier version of the road that was repurposed as a tunnel. No one appears to be quite sure. In any case, the concealed signs are an enticing glimpse at a London that is seldom seen.

KCYMAERXTHAERE
Bar Termini, 8 Old Compton Street, W1D 4TE

People love to contemplate alternative histories. What if the Roman Empire had survived? What if Napoleon or Hitler had won? Some take the concept much further. The brainchild of Eames Demetrios, Kcymaerxthaere (me neither) is 'a parallel universe that includes in its embrace our linear world – by which we mean our three dimensions of space – to the extent that places we encounter on what we call the Earth can become points of some kind of departure to these other realms'. To help spread the word, Demetrios deposits plaques in pertinent places to tell the stories of his fictitious universe. Old Compton St was the site of 'The Great Dangaroo Flood', and the plaque above Bar Termini marks its high waterline. The Tehachapi civilization endured 'two years at sea on their rafts of asphalt' before the floods receded, earning the British Isles their name of 'kNow Estrellia'; the joke being, presumably, that in this parallel world our rainy island has been colonized by the Antipodeans. This all sounds as if a *Game of Thrones* enthusiast has been to Amsterdam and eaten too much space cake, but why not go plaque hunting and decide for yourself? Other markers can be found all over the world and there are two more in London: De Laune St, Kennington, and Angel Alley, Whitechapel.

SWISS GLOCKENSPIEL
Swiss Court, W1D 6AP

Neutrality can be a good, if not always foolproof, method of keeping your relations cordial. Some say that fence-sitting is an admission of cowardice, but I doubt this applies to the Swiss. Julius Caesar's memoirs begin with the Helvetii deciding to invade France, and razing all their villages to the ground lest they get discouraged and head home. Little wonder that the Pope uses Swiss guards and no one has been brave enough to attack the place since Napoleon. Britain and Switzerland have close ties; both are reliant upon financial services, and the 'playground for the rich' model that London has adopted seems destined to make it Geneva without the scenery. A little piece of Switzerland was planted in London's West End in 1968, when the Swiss Centre opened on Wardour St. This modernist block housed Swiss restaurants and banks; it was intended to promote tourism and act as a focal point for Anglo–Swiss relations. In 1985 the Swiss added a glockenspiel to the centre, with cowbells and alpine figurines. Britain soon reciprocated by renaming the pedestrian cut-through to Leicester Square as Swiss Court. A 'cantonal tree', displaying the coats-of-arms of the twenty-six cantons in Switzerland, was erected. Despite these occasional efforts to keep the flame alive, the Swiss Centre fell out of favour; it was demolished in 2008. As a reminder of more innocent times, the glockenspiel was restored in a new, freestanding design. Its chimes, cows and shepherds now stand a few yards past the cantonal tree, underneath a smart, four-sided and presumably Swiss clock. Where the Swiss Centre stood you will now find M&M world, whose four floors of merchandise promote the bizarre devotional cult of anthropomorphized shell-coated chocolates. It is hugely successful.

BRYDGES PLACE
WC2N 4HP

Blink and you will miss Brydges Place. Fifteen inches wide at its tightest, this alleyway is usually referred to as the narrowest in London, although some confer the honour upon Emerald Court, Holborn. Brydges Place runs along the south side of the Coliseum, home to the English National Opera. You will probably have to squeeze past smokers from the Harp pub and the private members' club at No. 2. I am not aware of anyone having got stuck in the alley, but it may be worth checking that no one is coming in the opposite direction. It is well worth catching a show at the Coliseum, which tends to be slightly less traditional than the Royal Opera House. If the opera does not keep your attention, there's always the eye-watering décor, which sees every inch of wall and ceiling plastered with allusions to the Roman Empire. A statue has an amphitheatre stagehand about to unchain rampant lions, giant coins feature Caesar and Pompey, eagle standards and military friezes are recurring motifs. The effect is similar to entering a teenage girl's bedroom that has been converted into a shrine to One Direction.

HYDE PARK CORNER

QUADRIGA
Wellington Arch, Apsley Way, W1J 7JZ

Hyde Park Corner was traditionally considered the gateway to central London and the Duke of Wellington's London home there, Apsley House, had as its original address 'No.1, London'. The nearby Wellington Arch may be stuck, lamentably, on a traffic island, but as traffic islands go it is an eminent one. Decimus Burton built the arch in 1826 to celebrate the Duke's victory over Napoleon. Originally, the arch was home to a forty-ton equestrian statue of Wellington but it was hopelessly out of proportion. Everyone found it ugly and ridiculous, with the inconvenient exception of a delighted Wellington himself. He threatened to resign from all his official posts when the government wanted to remove it, and Queen Victoria reluctantly vetoed their decision. When the Duke died, his statue could finally be taken down. It now resides in Aldershot, while a smaller representation now stands a few metres from the triumphal arch, facing towards Apsley House. The spectacular quadriga, added to the top of the arch in 1912, is Europe's largest bronze. A small boy, barely visible, drives forward four galloping horses; behind, the winged figure of Nike is about to place a laurel wreath on his head. To stand under the huge Corinthian columns of the arch is to feel that the rampant horses are about to plunge over the edge and crush anyone in their path. It is a rather vertiginous experience. Another equestrian Duke of Wellington, in Glasgow's Royal Exchange Square, is famed for wearing a traffic cone on its head. Glasgow Council claim to spend £10,000 a year removing the cones, which Glaswegians replace as soon as they come off.

PORTER'S REST
Piccadilly, W1J 7NW

One of the most charming pieces of street furniture that I had marked out for inclusion in this book vanished quite suddenly and in mysterious circumstances. The porter's rest was a long wooden slab, standing at shoulder height on two iron poles, towards the end of Piccadilly. It was installed in

1861 to provide a few seconds' respite for porters carrying suitcases to the hotels of Park Lane and Knightsbridge. In 2014, the bench disappeared. Concerned citizens uncovered a Westminster Council document that authorized its removal with the Kafkaesque euphemisms much beloved by local government: following an 'internally generated' complaint, the bench was deemed a 'general nuisance'. This naturally caused outrage. Peter Berthoud, expert on the Soho noses, started a petition, alerting the media. The council soon backtracked and said that the porter's rest had simply gone missing, perhaps stolen, 'but we can't be certain'. Was it a cloak-and-dagger job by the council, or was the rest a victim of the epidemic of scrap-metal theft? Westminster mumbled platitudes about trying to find it or possibly installing a replacement, but few will be placing bets against the forces of inertia. In the meantime, there is a delightful 1940s clip of the bench in action here: http://www.britishpathe.com/video/porters-bench/query/Piccadilly.

HARRY NILSSON'S FLAT
1 Curzon Square, W1J 7FZ

There is a very awkward video of David Bowie and Bing Crosby's 1977 collaboration on 'Little Drummer Boy', where they stand before a fire making stilted, mutually suspicious small talk. 'I don't suppose you ever listen to any of the old fellows?', Bing enquires of Dave, who replies 'I do like that bloke with the beard . . . what's his name? Oh yeah, Harry Nilsson'. Chiefly remembered for 'Without You' or the *Midnight Cowboy* theme, Harry Nilsson was a prolific singer with a formidable discography to his name. His hedonistic lifestyle helped create some joyously great music, but saw him dogged by misfortune. Nilsson was John Lennon's companion on his eighteen-month 'lost weekend', and became something of a recluse after Lennon's murder. He owned a flat in Mayfair, close to his favourite London nightclubs, which friends were welcome to borrow. It was in this flat that Mama Cass of the Mamas & the Papas died in 1974; urban myth attributes her death to a ham sandwich, but the rotund chanteuse had fatally weakened her heart with a series of crash diets. Lightning struck a second time in 1978, when Keith Moon of the Who was using the flat. Moon died after a dinner of steak, champagne and thirty-two sleeping pills. Both musicians died in the bedroom, both at the age of thirty-two. A shaken Nilsson put the flat up for sale immediately and never returned. The ill-starred property, on the third floor of a Georgian townhouse, is still there today, although its address has changed from 9 Curzon Place to 1 Curzon Square. The handsome house is marred only by a clumsy bay window extension for a lift shaft, and its bricks are aptly black. It is not known whether any rock stars are fearless enough to stay the night these days.

KGB LAMPPOST
2 Audley Square, W1K 1HF

Walking up Audley St in Mayfair, one could easily miss Audley Square, which is hardly a square at all. The road widens a little bit on one side, accommodating four parking spaces, two townhouses and an eyesore of a multi-storey car park. Phones 4U billionaire John Caudwell has bought the car park, which he plans to demolish and replace with – you guessed it – luxury flats. Before the car park, outside No. 2, a lamppost has a small door that can be opened, and during the Cold War Soviet spies would use this as a drop-off point for letters, cassettes and small parcels. A chalk mark on the lamppost base would indicate a delivery. This secret was revealed by Oleg Gordievsky, a KGB colonel who was disenchanted by the quashing of the Prague Spring in 1968 and became a double agent for the West. Found out by Moscow, he evaded his chaperone guards during a morning jog and caught a train to the Finnish border, where he was able to defect. Coincidentally, while genuine secret-agent activity was taking place on the street, Cubby Broccoli was using 3 Audley Square to cast actors for Dr No, the first James Bond film. The building before the square, 1 South Audley St, is a lovely house in red sandstone which features an array of fearless putti boxing with dragons. It is depressing to note that this house is currently the Qatari embassy.

KNIGHTSBRIDGE

THE RUSSIAN ORTHODOX CHURCH
67 Ennismore Gardens, SW7 1NH

This small basilica is the base of the Russian Orthodox faith in the British Isles. Knowing Orthodox churches, and knowing one of the world's most affluent neighbourhoods, one enters expecting to be blinded by gold and colourful Byzantine icons. Instead, you find a neo-medieval Arts and Crafts affair, not a style commonly associated with churches. The aisles are marked off by two arcades of Romanesque arches, the roundels filled with lovely sgraffito depictions of Old and New Testament scenes. Twenty-one saints (plus two Holy Innocents and the Venerable Bede) populate the clerestory above, while foliage and twisting grape vines permeate the gaps. Some of the captions read like slightly eccentric proclamations ('He was bruised for our iniquities') but it is a thrilling accomplishment by artist Heywood Sumner. The apse is all gold gilding and its wall is clad in mother-of-pearl. The Church of England having packed up in 1955, the Russians moved in. With a congregation composed chiefly of White Russian émigrés and converts from High Anglicanism, the church was left to its own devices until the fall of Communism but Russia has since taken charge. The pews have been stripped out and the familiar painted iconostasis installed, but a heady mix of influences from Constantinople, Italy and Victorian

England has produced a church as cosmopolitan as the surrounding district.

SOUTH KENSINGTON

BÉLA BARTÓK STATUE
Onslow Square, SW7 3HU

The great Hungarian author Antal Szerb said of Britain that 'the sun rarely shines in these islands, but when it does the effect is so wonderful, it is as if it were smiling down on a new-created world'. Hungary and Britain have frequently exerted a two-way influence upon each other. Ernő Goldfinger designed some of London's finest tower blocks, while the Britons who built Budapest's Chain Bridge (based on Hammersmith Bridge) are still heroes in the Magyar capital. A small piece of Hungary can be found in Kensington in the form of a bronze statue of Béla Bartók. One of the twentieth century's major composers, he is as cherished for his tireless collection of endangered folk music in central Europe, Turkey and North Africa as for his *Concerto for Orchestra*. Hands deep in pockets, Bartók looks alert and slightly gaunt. Sporting a long coat and trilby hat, he stands on a stainless-steel pile of fallen leaves, a tiny bird at his feet. Compared with many statues in London, this one has a sprightly and unassuming quality, more Peter Pan than George V. It stands a few metres from South Kensington station and looks down Onslow Square towards 7 Sydney Place, where the composer always stayed when performing in London.

ALLEGORICAL LADIES
The Oratory, Brompton Road, SW7 2RP

Any of the many young Italians in London, should they be struck with homesickness, could do worse than pop into Brompton Oratory, a lavish Catholic church in the Italian style. A slightly muted neoclassical façade obscures the dome, but step inside and an explosion of décor parades before your eyes. Strolling through the yellow marble, statues and paintings of this dark and atmospheric place, it is hard to believe that you will not be stepping onto a piazza in Naples or Rome when you leave. It has elements of Renaissance and baroque – there are golden mosaics under the dome and rich tapestries covering the pilasters – and many components are Italian imports, such as an altar from Brescia and statues of the twelve apostles from Siena Duomo. The chapels are demarcated by round arches, and in a crowded field perhaps the most striking features are the statues of reclining ladies attached to the spandrels of these arches, underneath Latin text in huge gold lettering. We are used to carvings within spandrels but to have them in 3D is like reading a pop-up book. They appear to be allegorical, each clutching an object such as a set of scales, an anchor, or a martyr's palm. The Oratory is so unapologetically Italian that one imagines it must have put a few noses out of joint in the English establishment when it was built; they even do a swanky Latin mass. Interestingly, Cardinal Newman firmly opposed this location for the church, calling it 'a suburb . . . of second-rate gentry and second-rate shops' (how times change). Less opposed were Elgar, Hitchcock and Mallarmé, who all got married here.

MILESTONE
Royal Geographical Society, 1 Kensington Gore, SW7 2AR

On the outer walls of the Royal Geographical Society there is a milestone. It is around the height of a small child, painted with black text on white, and offers up the information that you are nine miles east of Hounslow and one mile west of London, and that it dates from 1911. It is strange to think that so recently in London's past somewhere as central as Kensington could have been considered outside its boundaries. It also strikes me as extremely late in the day to have installed a milestone, which we associate with period-drama characters making long journeys on horse and cart, or on foot if they are unlucky. Milestones go much further back than that; the Romans were in the habit of placing one every thousandth double-step, and the word mile derives from '*mille*', Latin for a thousand. Later on, milestones were important boundary markers. They finally became redundant in the automobile age. Many were defaced or removed in order to confuse the Germans in Hitler's invasion that never was, but a few thousand linger on, looked after by a society of enthusiasts.

MICHELIN RACING TILES
Michelin House, 81 Fulham Road, SW3 6RD

At some point in the twentieth century, Anglicanism was supplanted as the state religion of the UK by the motor car. In 1911, the Michelin Building on Fulham Rd became its first cathedral. Although a lifelong user of public transport who would happily see the back of the noisy pest that is the car, even I have to salute this building. There are very few in London with such buoyant swagger. Its façade is all tiles in lustrous white and spearmint green, the company name brandished in handsome art-deco lettering. Between the floors are ornamental ceramic friezes or garlanded tyres, and on each corner is an illuminated cupola in the form of stacked tyres. These innovations put architecture at the service of marketing. The curved gable houses a large, stained-glass Michelin Man; holding aloft a glass and captioned '*Nunc est bibendum*' (Now is the time to drink), this carries a faintly blasphemous echo of the Last Supper. The façade is such an audacious triumph that one could miss the vivacious tiles along the sides of the building, which depict the victories of cyclists and early racing drivers who used Michelin tyres. These are art nouveau, bordered by curling brown leaves, and great fun. They start with a man cycling from Paris to Brest in 1891, continuing to 1908. You can see the car's development from a cumbersome 'horseless carriage' to a sleek, streamlined racing machine. The green fields of Flanders are punctuated by farmhouses and distant spires, the Alps loom on the horizon as cars head south, and a race in Nice skirts the brilliant blue of the Mediterranean. The dashing drivers wear goggles, their cravats tailing in the breeze. Sir Terence Conran bought the building in 1987 and opened a restaurant named after Bibendum – the Michelin Man's official name. In 1991, Michelin sued the Scottish singer Momus for releasing a song about the Michelin Man's sexual prowess.

Victoria Line

The Victoria line was almost called the Viking line – not because it allows the people of Brixton and Walthamstow to carry out swift and brutal raids on the West End, but because it connects Victoria to King's Cross. It was conceived as a faster alternative to the Piccadilly line and covers much of the same ground with far fewer stops, allowing trains to reach higher speeds. Starting at the presently gentrifying Walthamstow, it serves north London, Bloomsbury and the West End before going south of the river to terminate at Brixton, which has changed as rapidly as Walthamstow, due in no small part to the Victoria line. Built in the 1960s, this line is less aesthetically pleasing than some of the others, and to compare its stations with those of the Piccadilly line is to see the bite of post-war austerity. The Victoria line is, however, enlivened by mosaics and tile illustrations on its platforms. Finsbury Park has hot-air balloons and duelling pistols, Tottenham Hale shows a ferryman at work and Stockwell has a rather modernist 'dazzle ship' depiction of a swan. Vauxhall gave the Russian language the word '*voksal*', meaning railway station. Just outside Finsbury Park there is a stretch where the trains sometimes run side by side for a few seconds; looking into the train that has suddenly appeared beside your own can feel like an out-of-body experience.

TOTTENHAM HALE

BRUCE CASTLE CLOCK TOWER
Bruce Castle Museum, Lordship Lane, N17 8NU

Tottenham is an impoverished, gang-heavy outpost of north London in which the 2011 riots originated. Most of its visitors flock to White Hart Lane stadium to watch the household names of Tottenham Hotspur. On the opposite side of the High St, within the grounds of a small park you will find the incongruous Bruce Castle, a stately home from the sixteenth century. This misleading name is purely the product of a previous owner's social climbing. Not quite a castle, its connection to the Bruce clan is equally tenuous: Robert the Bruce forfeited this land in 1306 upon accession to the Scottish throne. The oldest part of Bruce

Castle is Tudor, a round tower standing apart from the main building, thought to date from the reign of Henry VIII. The house has been added to and subtracted from for centuries, its best adornments coming from a makeover in 1684. The entrance forms the base of an impressive clock tower, clad in pink stucco. The square tower has balconies at two levels and is topped by an octagonal glass cupola, a bell and a weathervane. Bruce Castle could make a home fit for an underachieving £100,000-a-week footballer, but happily the building is currently a museum which houses Haringey Council's archives.

FINSBURY PARK

GHOST PLATFORMS
Parkland Walk, Florence Road, N4 3EY

Until 1954, the Great Northern Railway ran a suburban branch service from Finsbury Park to Alexandra Palace. In a rare reversion of the norm, mankind has relinquished its gains and handed the tracks back to the wild. Today, the Parkland Walk is a secluded, wooded dirt track covering the two miles between Finsbury Park and Highgate, much beloved of joggers and amateur filmmakers. There are still a few platforms where the trains used to stop, now swamped with moss, weeds and nettles. The tracks long gone, the platforms look bereft as they stare across at each other, entirely divorced from their original function. Could the flight of steps at either end be ziggurats leading to the sacrificial altars of a vanished civilization? The post-apocalyptic feel is spooky and evocative. Ultravox founder John Foxx walked it for inspiration when recording his masterpiece *Metamatic*, and Stephen King conceived the horror story 'Crouch End' after a visit. Look out for the 'green man' of sculptor Marilyn Collins, which emerges from a wall behind one platform. All sorts of scandalous goings-on are rumoured to happen here after dark; proceed with caution.

MILKING MURALS
The Old Dairy, 1–3 Crouch Hill, N4 4AP

If today's put-upon dairy farmers were to see the pastoral arcadia presented on the walls of the Old Dairy pub, I doubt they would recognize any of it. The gastropub is to be found where Stroud Green Rd becomes Crouch Hill, and is a joyless place chiefly concerned with speed dating, life classes and the provision of £13 burgers. Its exterior is, however, well preserved. Swirling gables, a pair of cupolas and cows' heads in garlands mark its red-and-white façade. Between Ionic pilasters is a sequence of seven ceramic murals, using the sgraffito technique. These illustrations have their origin in the early nineteenth century when much of Islington was still countryside, dotted with dairy farms that provided London with milk and butter. The Old Dairy was opened by the Friern Manor Dairy Company in 1836 and still functioned as a dairy as late as 1968. The murals, dating from the 1890s, present an idyllic image of the milk-making process that is slightly dishonest, as Friern Manor was pioneering industrial techniques at the time. The two-tone colouring is reminiscent of Japanese woodcuts. The scenes are populated with docile cows and, carrying jugs and pails, sturdy milkmaids who might have posed for Vermeer. The processes of grazing, milking, cooling, making butter and three forms of delivery are depicted. Having admired the murals, if you can postpone your well-earned pint there are good views to be had from the summit of Crouch Hill.

TURRETS AND TOWERS
Castle Climbing Centre, Green Lanes, N4 2HA

Next time you drop into Stoke Newington's Clissold Park to say hello to the deer, take a look north-west, and you will be transported back to an age when disinterested aristocrats ruled this fiefdom with benevolence, and the Hackney/Islington/Haringey borders were subjected to cattle raids from the Clan MacIvor. Green Lanes only comes to life past Manor House, where it forms the spine of the Haringey Ladder; but no, you are not dreaming. Right in the middle of a dull and empty stretch of the road, those are the turrets of what purports to be a medieval castle poking over the foliage. The castle sits adjacent to two reservoirs, and in 1855 it was built as a pumping station in the wake of the Clean Water Act. The crazy inspiration to build a castle for the station is a happy combination of two factors: at the time, the area was still bucolic countryside and it was felt that a huge industrial building would be dissonant. Meanwhile, the architect given the commission was about to retire and decided he might as well go out with a bang. An artificial mound was constructed for the castle to sit on, giving the impression that it was surrounded by a moat, and its parapets even include gaps for archers. Most commentators describe the style as 'Scottish baronial' and detect the influence of Stirling Castle, but others liken it to the Crusader fortresses built in Acre and Antioch. The clever thing is that the exterior is not mere ornament. Each tower is a different shape, size or height, but each one is earning its crust. One is a chimney shaft, one contains the main water tank, and the conical turret has stairs for workmen to access the roof. By 1971, the station was obsolete and the water board applied to demolish the castle. What to do with a fake castle? Proving that truth is stranger than fiction, in 1994 it was made into a climbing school, and remains so today.

HIGHBURY & ISLINGTON

HIGHBURY SQUARE
Avenell Road, N5 1FE

'Highbury is a library', football crowds used to sing. It's even quieter now that the erstwhile Arsenal stadium is a gated-access enclave of flats where prices start at £500,000. The Veuve Clicquot drinkers of Arsenal FC relocated here from Woolwich in 1913 and left again in 2006 when they built a new 60,000-seater Emirates Stadium off Holloway Rd. The Highbury ground's East and West stands, built in the thirties, are listed structures for their art-deco looks and the blocks were converted into residential property, the pitch into landscaped gardens. The turnstiles are gone but the neatly symmetrical stands are still in the club colours of red and white, and emblazoned with 'Arsenal Stadium' in giant lettering. It is an understated design, especially when compared to the *Close Encounters* grandiosity of the Emirates, and the reassignment does not attempt to hide the original function. The Gunners' former star Robert Pirès snapped up one flat. The cube-shaped glass fronts that face onto the pitch suggest that all the terraces have been replaced by executive boxes, which is slightly chilling for dyed-in-the-wool football supporters. In 2012, Arsenal raised the prices of their best seats to £126 a game.

KING'S CROSS ST PANCRAS

THE MEETING PLACE
St Pancras International, N1C 4QP

The couple in Paul Day's sculpture *The Meeting Place* would be nauseating enough were they in the flesh and to scale, but that they stand nine metres tall magnifies the horror. The girl strokes her lover's face as his arms enfold her waist, and the rucksack on his back implies that he could be a demobbed soldier, but there is something reptilian about their blank, elongated eyes. One wag remarked that the pair look as if they have had a mortgage application rejected. Antony Gormley called this 'a very good example of the crap out there', and he should know. If this is democratic, populist art, give us abstract squiggles. Somewhat better is the clay frieze added to the round base of the bronze in 2008. Labourers lay down tracks in a tunnel. Soldiers on a train wave goodbye to stricken-looking women and children; behind are returning soldiers, their eyes heavily bandaged. Some people kiss, grope and rub against each other with abandon, while more bashful suitors steal glances from behind their books. The bronze coating has rubbed off on a dog that people have taken to petting. The frieze had to be modified after the *Daily Mail* led an outcry against some components: a drunken tramp about to fall under a train driven by the Grim Reaper, and a copulating couple. Dullards complained about the 'bad taste', yet made no objection to the monstrosity above. Easier to like is the statue of John Betjeman, who saved the station, a few paces away. The poet's coat-tails are flapping in the breeze as he holds down his hat and gazes up, as if awestruck, at the engineering feat that is the vast single-span roof.

CARYATIDS
St Pancras Church of England, Euston Road, NW1 2BA

Built in 1819–22, just as Bloomsbury began to take off, the lofty Greek revival style of St Pancras New Church brings a touch of stateliness to the perpetually traffic-heavy Euston Rd. Ionic columns support a weighty pediment at the front with an apse at the rear. The most distinctive feature of the church is a pair of porticoes that supplement either side, through which the crypt is accessed. Each is held up by four rather Amazonian ladies, whose larger-than-life proportions exaggerate their broad noses, slightly unkempt locks and stern frowns; the latter may be directed at the traffic that has bequeathed them a coating of soot. The caryatids hold extinguished torches and empty jugs to indicate that they are watching over a burial vault. Many visitors find the figures slightly dumpy, and a popular legend has it that they were built a few inches too tall to fit into the space provided; akin to a performing magician, the sculptor removed a section of their midriffs. At the British Museum, you can, for the time being, see one of the original Athenian caryatids that inspired those on the church; twenty-two centuries older, she was brought to London by Lord Elgin.

HARDY TREE
St Pancras Gardens, Pancras Road, NW1 1UL

Squeezed into a slender strip of land between the busy Pancras Rd, the train tracks, the canal, a hospital and the council flats of Somers Town, it is a surprise to find this ancient church and its verdant gardens, looking like they belong to a Dorset village. Restored from a derelict state over the course of the nineteenth and twentieth centuries, St Pancras Old Church has never been accurately dated. The church itself alludes to one theory that it was a Roman temple, consecrated as a church in 314 CE. Like the oldest English churches, its walls are stocked with plaques, icons and ecclesiastical bric-a-brac. The attractive churchyard is similarly rich in historical pickings. Sir John Soane's enigmatic mausoleum, with its marble canopy over four columns, inspired George Gilbert Scott's classic design for the red London phone box. Mary Wollstonecraft is buried here and her daughter Mary met Shelley, the romantic poet, here to plan their elopement. Another literary connection is the ash tree encircled by a tight huddle of gravestones, the work of a young Thomas Hardy. In 1865, a large slice of the churchyard had to be excavated to make way for the train tracks entering St Pancras station. While working as an architect's assistant, Hardy was given the grisly task of dismantling those tombs in the way and rehousing the remains within. To help dispose of the headstones, an ash tree was planted and a number of stones packed in circular formation around its base. The stones are intertwined with the roots of the tree, and some became embedded into the tree trunk – in the midst of death, life. Not that Hardy relished the task of disturbing the dead. His poem 'The Levelled Churchyard' finds their bones 'mixed to human jam/And each exclaims to each in fear/I know not which I am!' The total loss of individual characteristics is one of the most alarming things about seeing catacomb skeletons. Pondering one's fate was evidently a preoccupation for Hardy. Turning his hand to fiction, he was not shy about passing on his bad luck to characters such as *Tess of the D'Urbervilles* or *Jude the Obscure*, and the rest is history.

FAIRY TALES
Sidney Estate, Werrington Street, NW1 1QP

In the twenty-first century, all of inner London is Billionaire's Row. The tiniest flats can fetch seven figures and the idea of a home in Zone 1 is now reserved for fairy-tale reveries. When we were building council housing instead of demolishing or selling it, the dream was a reality for some. Somers Town is a pocket of council housing between Euston, St Pancras and Bloomsbury, the continued existence of which seems as improbable as that of Asterix's village. Around the corner from the Eurostar terminal, it feels twenty miles away. At its heart is the Sidney Estate, completed in 1938. The blocks face a central courtyard. As if demonstrating their commitment to high quality, each block has lunette panels over central windows with depictions of fairy tales, courtesy of Gilbert Bayes. The stories are chiefly from Hans Christian Andersen and the Brothers Grimm, and deceptively barbed. We see princes, princesses, mermaids, knights and swans, but look up 'The Goose Girl' or 'The Swineherd' and you find dark tales replete with violence and unhappy endings. Taking centre-stage in the courtyard is a wonderful clock face surrounded by putti representing the four seasons, each appropriately clothed (or not) and bearing seasonal produce. In the side courtyards, even the posts for washing lines were decorated by Bayes; those by St Nicholas Flats have jaunty little sailing ships. In Edwardian times, Somers Town included some of the worst slums in London, with many families confined to a single room. A blue plaque on this estate marks the achievements of Father Basil Jellicoe, who founded the St Pancras Housing Association and was an indefatigable fundraiser for decent homes.

WARREN STREET

JEREMY BENTHAM AUTO-ICON
University College London, Gower St, WC1E 6BT

Faced with their own mortality, the thinkers of the Enlightenment often felt it necessary to put their money where their mouths were and show a cavalier disregard for superstition. On his deathbed, Hume told Boswell that it would be 'a most unreasonable fancy that we should exist forever'. The unconventional arrangements made by Jeremy Bentham, the founder of Utilitarianism, could be seen as a gift to science, a joke on death, or a whim that reveals a subconscious desire for eternal life. Upon his death in 1832, friends dissected his corpse in public (dissection was still frowned upon) and made an 'auto-icon' of his body. It was placed within his own clothes, padded out with hay and put behind glass in a cabinet, where Bentham sits with some of his personal effects: a cane and glasses. The exhibit has been kept in the South Cloisters of University College London since

1850. Bentham wished for his head to be mummified but attempts at the Maori method of desiccation were botched, and the result looked gruesome. The head soon came apart from the skeleton and was placed between his feet, replaced on the icon by a wax likeness of Bentham, which used some of his own hair. It was kidnapped by students from the local rivals, King's College London, in 1975, and there are various urban myths about uncouth students borrowing it for use as a football. The head is now kept in a climate-controlled safe. Bentham's legacy extends beyond his physical remains. Utilitarianism gets a bad press for its focus on measurement and calculation (people think of Mr Gradgrind from *Hard Times*) but many of Bentham's beliefs have since become mainstream. He was against the death penalty but for social reform, individual liberty, legalizing homosexuality, and the separation of church and state.

GREEN PARK

UNUSED ARCHWAY
Marlborough House, Pall Mall, SW1Y 5HX

As well as being Britain's wealthiest woman, Sarah Churchill, Duchess of Marlborough, was a favourite and close confidante of Queen Anne. She consistently used her influence to further the cause of the Whigs, and the relationship was a source of innuendo for the resentful. Her house is tucked in behind the southern side of Pall Mall. It was built by Wren in 1711, although his uncluttered design has been subjected to new floors and extensions over the years. The general impression is one of cosy luxury, yet its forecourt displays the residue of a personal vendetta. One of the Duchess's many enemies was Robert Walpole, who had been her husband's clerk and went on to become generally regarded as the very first prime minister. An archway in the central wall was intended to give the Duchess direct access onto Pall Mall. Out of spite, Walpole prevented her plans by quickly buying up the land in front. To this day, the house is hidden behind the buildings on Pall Mall and accessed through a slightly circuitous route from a side gate. Right up against the rear of the Oxford and Cambridge Club and hidden behind foliage, the elegant central arch leads nowhere. It looks like a slightly embarrassed guest to the party who has taken a wrong turning and ended up in the linen cupboard. George V's Queen Mary spent her widowhood living here, and since her death it has housed the Commonwealth Secretariat.

TEXAN EMBASSY
Pickering Place, SW1A 1EA

The secluded Pickering Place at the heart of St James's, across the road from the Carlton Club, is said to be the smallest square in Britain. It still uses gaslight and the pretty Georgian buildings surround a small courtyard with flowers, plants and a little sundial at its centre. Famous residents have included Graham Greene and twice prime minister Lord Palmerston. The square was built by Berry Bros. & Rudd, London's oldest wine merchants, who have been here since 1698. Before it became Pickering Place, the site hosted a medieval leper colony and later became Henry VIII's tennis courts. The unaltered square feels terribly genteel today, but St James's was once rather livelier. Concealed places tend to attract vice and although one might struggle to swing a cat in Pickering Place, it was a popular venue for cockfights, dogfights, gambling and bare-knuckle boxing. One of the many to have contested a duel in the square was the famous dandy Beau Brummell. All this implies that it would make a good home for a cowboy, and so it proved when the fledgling Republic of Texas had its embassy here. Texas had declared independence from Mexico in 1836 and during a brief but colourful existence, it fought bloody battles with both Mexicans and Comanches. At the top of the covered alley leading off St James's St, a brass plaque marks the site of the 'Texas Delegation' until 1845, at which point the republic joined the United States. Just as the likes of Britain and Spain long to balkanize themselves, oil-rich Texans still make the occasional threat to secede from the superpower.

VICTORIA

ST ANDREW'S CHAPEL
Westminster Cathedral, 42 Francis Street, SW1P 1QW

An arriviste among our cathedrals, Britain's largest Catholic church did not open until 1903. It's a vast, stripy, exotic thing with broad and shallow domes. The cupola that crowns the cloud-chasing campanile turns it into a bishop's staff. The façade is a dreamlike array of first-floor arcades and dome-topped polygonal towers; the whole thing looks more like the Byzantine Hagia Sophia in Istanbul than Roman. In 2014 a minor UKIP politician was ridiculed when he mistook the Cathedral for a mosque, but you can see why he did so. The interior is cavernous and dimly lit. It feels halfway between a mystical, spiritual place redolent of the early Church, and an upmarket kitchen showroom; marble in every colour under the sun, and lots of it. British Catholic churches, next to their continental neighbours, can feel like a new pair of leather shoes not yet broken in. Here, many of the mosaics are pastel-coloured and the figures have a cartoon quality: the ox, eagle, lion and man above the altar have something of My Little Pony about them. The right-hand side aisle contains chapels for the saints and people of Scotland, Ireland and Wales. Westminster Cathedral is at its best when at its most Byzantine, and in a nod to St Andrew's Levantine origins, the Scottish chapel has some magnificent San Vitale-style mosaics.

The arches are filled with Celtic patterns and vines from a plant pot, with doves resting here and there. Between the round arches, the spandrels contain recognizable, postcard views of six cities relevant to the saint's life, including Patras in Greece and his hometown, the fishing village of Bethsaida. There is a wonderful view of Constantinople, with Hagia Sophia at the centre, its dome and surrounding rooftops glittering gold as distant lights twinkle in the city's outskirts. On the other side are the three places that received Andrew's relics: Milan's Sant' Ambrogio, Amalfi's Duomo and, at the centre, St Andrew's itself. Grassy hills jut into the sea, with sandy beaches between. Pointedly, cottages huddle around the great cathedral that went to ruin after the Reformation. The chapel of Holy Souls, dedicated to those in purgatory, is also intriguing. Mosaics show angels holding hell-hounds on leashes, while flames lap around people writhing and clutching their faces.

LEWD WINDOWS
Albert Tavern, 52 Victoria Street, SW1H 0NP

When unsavoury characters in London pubs invite you back to see their etchings, the windows at this tavern are, I fear, exactly the sort of thing they're on about. Victoria St is a largely unattractive street dominated by glass high-rises with one or two gems. One of these is the Albert Tavern, which was built in 1862 and managed to survive both the Blitz and the fashion for converting pubs into bars. It has many period features, and there is even a division bell to summon MPs out of their stupor when their presence is required down the road. The decorations etched onto the frosted-glass windows are particularly striking. Some people can see the image of a particular action, covertly smuggled into the pattern, which is far too obscene to merit description in a respectable tome such as this. Let's say that it is believed to demonstrate the prowess and potency of the Prince Consort who gave the pub its name. Said to have been a prudish sort, Albert nonetheless fathered nine children. Compared with the arguably over-the-top Albert Memorial and Royal Albert Hall, these windows are a coarse and unsanctioned relic of the Victorian age; and yet, like the piercing that also carries his name, they might say more about Prince Albert's ill-defined role and how he was perceived by the public. Don't worry if, like me, you spend a long time staring at the windows without seeing anything untoward (a clue: look just under the larger crests with birds and butterflies inside). We are all in the gutter, but not all of us have our minds down there.

WINGS OVER THE WORLD
157–197 Buckingham Palace Road, SW1W 9SP

In the 1920s and 1930s, Imperial Airways was a predecessor to British Airways, whose flying boats connected all the pink parts of the globe. Completed in 1939, its London terminal beside Victoria station gave passengers a rail link to the aircraft at Southampton. It was a forerunner to the modern-day airport terminal, and is an accomplished piece of art deco. Either side of a clock tower are two five-storey wings that curve gently inwards. The National Audit Office is based there now; the original name may have been expunged from above the doorway, but sufficient discretion has been shown to leave Eric Broadbent's *Speed Wings Over the World* sculpture. Two winged figures cradle a large globe, their outstretched arms joining under a miniature pair of wings in the foreground. It nods to antiquity but adds thrust, excitement and a sense of motion, as would have befitted this revolutionary method of transport. Travel was still glamorous and elegant in those days and city-centre termini ensured that the airline would leave you right at your destination. Today, the airline deposits you at a rural shed, where you must sit on your suitcase until a Terravision coach carries you the final seventy miles into town.

PIMLICO

PAOLOZZI VENTILATION TOWER
Pimlico Station, Bessborough Road, SW1V 2JA

As Crossrail hurtled towards completion, Tottenham Court Road station was given a substantial makeover. In early 2015, art lovers were horrified to discover that the station had been stripped of its vivid mosaics by Eduardo Paolozzi; the less public art there is, the more room for advertising. Admirers of Paolozzi can still get their fix by exiting the Underground at Pimlico. Before they get to the Tate Britain or Thomas Cubitt's streets of white stucco houses, travellers will be confronted with an object seemingly at war with its neighbours. Erected in 1982, this covering for an air vent is reminiscent of a robot from 1960s sci-fi, a vaguely humanoid form whose curved pipes resemble limbs. Abstract reliefs on the lower part of the sculpture depict cogs, clocks, levers and other components that will look familiar to anyone who has been faced with a photocopier paper jam. Modern in tooth and claw, the sculpture opts not to disguise its industrial function, but to broadcast and champion it. Other notable Paolozzi pieces in London include a large *Sir Isaac Newton* outside the British Library and a giant segmented head outside the Design Museum near Tower Bridge.

VAUXHALL

BROWN DOG
Battersea Park, SW11 4NJ

Battersea Park is a huge green lung on the South Bank. Before the park was laid out, the Duke of Wellington came here to fight a duel with pistols. Its 200 acres contain many amenities; strolling along Chelsea Embankment, it's a surprise to see a vast pagoda across the river, with four plump Buddhas sitting in its niches. Another curious artefact to be found in the park is a statue marking the Brown Dog Affair, a cause célèbre that raged through Edwardian Britain for seven years. A group of Swedish anti-vivisectionists attended an eminent doctor's UCL lecture, at which a dog was dissected. In the doctor's version of events, the dog had been heavily anaesthetized and did not suffer; according to the Swedes, it was visibly struggling and terrified. The doctor successfully sued for libel, but the matter did not end there. Mark Twain published a short story written from the perspective of the pup, and campaigners placed a dog statue (complete with fountains on two levels, for people and animals, and a provocatively worded plaque) in Battersea, known for its dogs' home. *The New York Times* called the plaque 'hysterical' and 'a slander', and 'anti-doggers' were so incensed that the statue became a target for vandalism. The dog had to be placed under twenty-four-hour guard. Three thousand medical students marched on the statue and Battersea's residents sprang to its defence, leading to the 'Brown Dog Riots'. Defying public opinion, the local council decided enough was enough and had the statue melted down. In 1985 a new dog was unveiled in Battersea Park, this time a terrier standing on a stone plinth with a more playful pose. Anxious not to reopen old wounds, the council soon moved it from its original location to the Old English Garden in the Woodland Walk.

ROYAL DOULTON WORKSHOP
Southbank House, Black Prince Road, SE1 7SJ

Lambeth High St is not much of a high street at all. This tranquil backwater contains one pub, a small park, a few scraps of council housing and the rear of the many tall buildings that face onto the Albert Embankment. However, carry on to the corner where it meets Black Prince Rd (the 'Black Prince' being Prince Edward, ruler of Aquitaine and scourge of the French), and you will run into a startling polychrome firework, two bays wide yet five storeys high (with a less showy extension on Black Prince Rd), and quite at odds with anything else around it. Around red brick, the terracotta patterns employ complementary shades from deep carnation pink to light and creamy beige, with the odd blue jewel used sparingly. The detail is immense. Small Corinthian columns support Gothic arches, tiny winged monsters hiss at you from above, and emerging from the corner is a florid oriel turret. Beneath this, the doorway tympanum features a splendid frieze of people in a workshop full of decorated jars. All becomes clear when you learn that this is the only surviving fragment of Royal Doulton's ceramics complex on the Albert Embankment. Business boomed as their glazed pipes were preferred to porous brick; their wares could also insulate electricity. In the 1860s they moved into decorative products, hiring the best graduates from the nearby Lambeth School of Art. The building we see today came in 1878, and its ornate exterior was clearly intended to show off their craftsmanship. The figures in the tympanum have been identified as portraits of the firm's most prominent artists, and the gesticulating, seated man is Henry Doulton himself. The only woman appears next to a vase with a lion, and a cat hides under her chair; this is Hannah Barlow, who specialized in animal portraits. The man holding a vase at the centre is George Tinworth, sculptor of the piece. The 1956 Clean Air Act obliged Royal Doulton to relocate to Stoke-on-Trent, and most of the Embankment buildings were demolished.

FIREMEN
London Fire Brigade Headquarters, Albert Embankment, SE1 7SP

Separated from the South Bank's cultural centres by St Thomas' Hospital and Lambeth Palace, the Albert Embankment may see far fewer visitors than most of its riverside neighbours, but it is not wholly devoid of charm. Its benches have swan armrests to match the

sphinx and camel benches on Victoria Embankment, and the International Maritime Organisation features a striking memorial: a vast ship's bow emerges from its lobby, a lone seaman standing at the prow. Opened in 1937, it is the London Fire Brigade (LFB) headquarters that dominates this stretch of the riverfront. Its nine storeys were presumably built to provide accommodation for London's firemen, and they look somewhat akin to the grand mansion flats found in north-west London. This vast building is not very big on ornament, but makes a few concessions to art deco. Gilbert Bayes and Nicholas Babb provided some stone reliefs of firemen at work: Bayes's three works, at the centre of the lower floors, are on a gold mosaic background. Mermen use spouting fish as impromptu hoses to douse a fire, and above are mythical monsters and a deity driving a chariot through a sunburst. Babb's two pieces on the ground floor are much more literal, but have a captivating drama. Three firemen use short ladders with hooks to ascend a burning building, tongues of flame escaping through its windows. On the plaque opposite, three firemen train their streams on the blaze while another busies himself unravelling the hoses. The LFB left Albert Embankment in 2007, but has recently contemplated returning to the vacant building. The failure of attempts to convert the premises into apartments for foreign investors might represent the only occasion this country has said no to the Qataris.

BRIXTON

NUCLEAR DAWN MURAL
Carlton Mansions, Coldharbour Lane, SW9 8QD

Brixton is one of London's livelier neighbourhoods. The post-war *Windrush* generation of Afro-Caribbean immigrants made Brixton a melting pot, and it has experienced periodical rioting from locals indignant at excessive police interference. It is now the kind of area to which people with trust funds move for its 'edge'. Brixton has consequently become a front line in the battle against the tide of gentrification, leading to further protests and clashes with the police. Following the 1981 riots, the council commissioned a series of colourful wall murals to promote peace and harmony. Some have gone or are in disrepair, but the survivors are worth looking at. Perhaps the most of-its-time mural is found just past the railway tracks on Coldharbour Lane. *Nuclear Dawn* shows a colossal skeleton standing over London, draped in the flags of the UK, the USA and the USSR. Like a farmer sowing seeds, the skeleton casts war planes that drop bombs on the city. Big Ben and Parliament are visible, but the bottom metre, which depicted Thatcher's cabinet in an underground shelter, has been covered by graffiti tags. The block of flats housing the mural has been earmarked for redevelopment. Already faded and vandalized, the mural's future seems as precarious as humanity's future would have seemed in the early eighties when the Cold War intensified. This mural was part of a wider effort to make the public aware of what was at stake. More cheering, if further to walk, is the *Big Splash* mural on Glenelg Rd, which features a water mill, an array of wildlife and children playing in an idealized open-air version of the subterranean Effra river.

Circle Line

One story, which I have always suspected was too good to be true, credits Stalin with the invention of the Circle line. The Moscow Metro was struggling with overcrowding and various planners were summoned to bring their solutions before the Soviet premier. An unimpressed Uncle Joe slammed down his coffee cup on the middle of a metro map, leaving a brown circle around the city centre. The planners realized that this was just what was needed. In London, the Circle line is a useful hop-on, hop-off route for interchange with other lines. Stretches of its tracks are the oldest in the Underground system: Paddington to Farringdon opened in 1863, and South Kensington to Westminster following in 1868. Aldgate station was built over a plague pit containing the remains of a thousand victims of the 1665 epidemic. The Circle was completed in 1884, before a five-year-old Stalin had even begun training for the priesthood. It is nearer the surface than most parts of the Underground, as workers used the cut-and-cover technique rather than digging tunnels, and several stretches of the line see daylight. *The Times* reported that the line was a 'torture which no person would undergo if he could conveniently help it' – carriages were originally windowless and earned the sobriquet 'padded cells'. The original joint-owners of the line's tracks, the Metropolitan Railway and the District Railway, failed to agree on the best way to run the line and so one ran the clockwise services and the other the anti-clockwise. The Circle line had to wait until 1949 before receiving its own colour on the Tube map. Its starting point is currently Edgware Road, on the fringe of the West End. It runs parallel to the Hammersmith & City and Metropolitan lines along the southerly edge of north London and into the City via Farringdon and Barbican, after which it follows the District line along the Thames before turning north into west London. Since 2009, the Circle line's circle has been broken by a branch that extends to Hammersmith and makes it more of a snail.

HIGH STREET KENSINGTON

THE ARAB HALL
Leighton House Museum, 11 Holland Park, W14 8LZ

The Victorian painter, sculptor and traveller Frederic Leighton had excellent establishment credentials. He was President of the Royal Academy, he is buried in St Paul's and his genteel, classically inspired paintings held no truck with modernism. His most enduring work, however, is his extraordinary house near Kensington High St. A garden-facing studio is immersed in light, burnished tiles of deep turquoise make the hallway feel like an aquarium, while upstairs a surprisingly spartan bedroom contains a small single bed. The centrepiece of the house is the Arab Hall, built to showcase his huge collection of antique tiles and stained glass from Syria, Iran and Turkey, many acquired on his behalf by Sir Richard Burton. Like a courtyard at the centre of a caravanserai, the four-sided room centres on a fountain. Everywhere you look, tiles in blue, white and green depict flowers, peacocks and Quranic quotations in Arabic, with De Morgan mosaics and tiling filling in the gaps. There are chaises longues in front of the bay-window shutters, and rich, pink marble pillars. Above, a wide chandelier hangs low from a tall golden dome with eight stained-glass windows around its base. Connoisseurs of eighties pop may recognize the room from the videos to 'Golden Brown' by the Stranglers and 'Gold' by Spandau Ballet. Lord Leighton is to be congratulated for getting any painting done when the temptation to sit here and smoke opium with the harem must have been strong.

KENSINGTON ROOF GARDENS
99 Kensington High Street, W8 5SA

London specializes in places that, despite being a stone's throw apart, seem like different worlds. Two such places are Kensington High St, perpetually congested with traffic and shoppers, and a few storeys up in the air, the hanging gardens of Kensington. No. 99 on the high street was originally Derry & Toms department store, which in the 1930s laid out a set of gardens on the acre-and-a-half of the roof. There is a garden in the style of Moorish Spain, a Tudor garden and an English woodland garden. The Spanish garden is best known, with its sugar-pink buildings and cute little towers. The others are more demure but contain trees, climbing plants and a small stream with fish. The gardens also boast a family of resident flamingos. You are at once far away from London and right in the thick of it. Altogether it feels much more like the Beverly Hills home of some twenties film star than an inner-city office block. The traffic below has been reduced to a gentle murmur and the only intrusion is the spire of nearby St Mary Abbots, disconcertingly close to head height. It is as hallucinatory an experience as coming across Portmeirion village on the deserted sands of north

Wales. The gardens are open to the public when not in use, but are a perennial venue for weddings, parties and promo launches. You are recommended to phone ahead on the day you wish to visit, and photo ID is required. Entrance is via the reception area on the Derry St side of the building.

WINGED LIONS
Baglioni Hotel, 60 Hyde Park Gate, SW7 5BB

Although I have never seen a winged lion in the flesh, they have been around for millennia if sculpture is anything to go by. The British Museum has some vast Assyrian lamassu, winged bulls or lions with human heads. These mythical beasts were seen as protectors in Babylonian culture. The image was taken up by the ancient Jews and eventually became the winged lion of St Mark the Evangelist. Where Kensington High St meets De Vere Gardens, a hotel has a set of small winged lions seated upright, their wings spread, and looking out from each corner. They look fairly wise and pensive, as lions go. Made of terracotta and installed in 1898, they were sculpted by Alfred Drury. Drury is best known for the more grandiose pieces on the entrance of the nearby Victoria and Albert

Museum, but these captivating lions show that the small, unaffected jobs are often where the magic resides. There is no historical anomaly or curious backstory to them. I include them for the simple reason that they are especially beautiful and, with Kensington Gardens for competition, could very easily be missed. When De Vere Gardens was laid out it was hoped that it would become one of London's grandest streets, but houses were slow to sell and many were converted into hotels or apartments; Henry James lived in a flat at No. 34.

NOTTING HILL GATE

PEOPLE'S HALL OF FRESTONIA
Freston Road, W11 4BD

South of the Westway, the triangle of land formed by Notting Hill's Bramley Rd, Freston Rd and Shalfleet Drive is not conspicuous; there are decent low-rise council flats, a few old houses, a converted brewery and arches for the railway line. The low-key environment makes the story of Frestonia all the better. Notting Hill already had a micronation precedent in G. K. Chesterton's *The Napoleon of Notting Hill*, which saw a quixotic hero form an army and defend his neighbourhood from a new motorway. In 1977, the aforementioned streets were occupied by some

120 squatters, whom the council hoped to evict. Inspired by the film *Passport to Pimlico*, the residents held a referendum on independence from the UK. When 94 per cent voted in favour, Frestonia was born. David Rappaport, who later played the Dwarf King in *Time Bandits*, was appointed Foreign Secretary and playwright Heathcote Williams was Frestonia's ambassador to Britain. Every resident adopted the surname Bramley, thus obliging the council to rehouse them together in the event of eviction. Frestonia applied to join the United Nations and lobbied for a UN peacekeeping force to be sent to W11. On the corner of Freston Rd and Olaf St, the People's Hall was their gathering place. Four storeys of red brick, it housed Frestonia's National Film Theatre and both the Clash and Motörhead recorded albums here. From the perspective of illiberal 2015, it is amazing to note that this wheeze managed to last five years – enough time for Frestonia to stave off the evictions and demolitions, and even receive some 'foreign aid' from the UK. Some of its families still live within the housing cooperative that was established. As London councils sell off their remaining estates and try to move tenants to Birmingham or Margate, the time may well be ripe for some new republics.

GREAT PORTLAND STREET

TRIUMPHAL ARCHES
Chester Terrace, NW1 4ND

All the self-assurance of the Enlightenment is here. The Outer Circle of Regent's Park is lined with plush neo-classical terraces, most of them designed in the Regency era by John Nash. Particularly remarkable are the buildings lining the eastern edge of the circle: the three Cs of Cambridge, Chester and Cumberland, each one grander than the last. Cumberland is pure Palladianism, its Ionic columns and creamy stucco front topped by dozens of classical statues in glossy white coats. Viewed from the park, the central pediment, whose frieze sees a huge cast crammed onto a celestial blue background, is bombastic to the brink of silliness. Step back and the pediment is gradually hidden by a tree, like a circumspect butler who intervenes when the drunken master makes a fool of himself. Chester Terrace is by comparison discreet, concealed behind trees and turning its back on the public park. To uncover its secrets, you must walk right up to it. Turning off the Circle at Chester Gate, you are confronted with the startling sight of towering triple arches at either end. They are big enough to commemorate a triumph for Augustus or Hadrian, and announce the name of Chester Terrace in mammoth white-on-blue block capitals. The arches make this rarefied terrace seem like a home for giants, and it is hard to conceive of the confidence required to emblazon your address on such a scale. Famous residents have included Sir Ralph Richardson and John Profumo.

BARBICAN

HOLY SEPULCHRE MODELS
Museum of the Order of St John, St John's Gate,
St John Street, EC1M 4DA

The medieval orders of knights can be tricky concepts to get our modern brains around; very powerful bodies at the time, most have either vanished or morphed into something quite different. Everyone knows the St John Ambulance and its familiar Maltese cross, but it is an eye-opener to realize how far back the organization goes. It began as Knights Hospitallers in Crusader Jerusalem, offering shelter and healthcare to poor pilgrims. When Jerusalem fell the knights moved to Acre and then Rhodes, which also fell, so Charles V allowed them to have the isle of Malta for a peppercorn rent. The knights built many of its towns, including the capital city of Valletta, and remained until ousted by Napoleon. The London headquarters of the order are based around a suitably antique city gate in Clerkenwell that dates from 1504, although much of its stone cladding was replaced by the

Victorians. Inside, a free museum uses original artefacts to illustrate the order's history: centuries-old guidebooks for pilgrims, armour and weaponry, and ceramics from Malta and the Islamic world. Particularly good are two models of Jerusalem's Church of the Holy Sepulchre, showing its domes and tower. They have been painstakingly assembled; one is in dark wood, the other studded with mother of pearl, and pieces of ivory on both form slender Romanesque arches. The various sections of the church look like exquisite jewellery boxes. In the seventeenth century, these would have made very upmarket souvenirs for the richest pilgrims.

SMITHFIELD DRAGONS
225 Central Markets, EC1A 9LH

The City of London's emblem is a silver dragon with red tongue and wings, posing with the City coat of arms. As you travel around London you will notice various small statues of this dragon, used as boundary markers along the edge of the City. They are odd creatures whose diminutive stature makes them look silly rather than fearsome. The curved wings resemble the shoulder pads of some veteran stadium rocker. With one front hoof resting on the heraldic shield and the other dangling limp, their pose is rather camp. To find a dragon with real bite, you must head to Smithfield Market. Walking between Barbican and Farringdon you cannot miss the market, a prominent and stylish piece of Victorian engineering. The current structure was built in 1866 to the design of Sir Horace Jones, also responsible for Leadenhall Market and Tower Bridge, but there has been a meat market here since the tenth century. In the decades after the Reformation it was a place of execution and forgers would be boiled in oil. The covered market has a copper dome at both ends and an arched avenue separating the two wings, with a four-sided clock and decorative iron supports painted turquoise and purple. Perching in the spandrels beneath each are properly fierce dragons who look ready to pounce on some of the produce, or punters, beneath. The edges of their wing span look sharp as claws, their backs have ridged plates, their tongues and tails are forked, and they look down on us with an intense glare; but so far, no sign of life.

THE OLDEST HOUSE IN LONDON
41 Cloth Fair, EC1A 7JQ

Down the narrow street next to St Bartholomew the Great are some exceedingly old houses. No. 41, looking onto the churchyard, was built in 1614. A group of eleven houses in this area, surrounded by priory walls on four sides, came through the Great Fire unscathed. This one is the only survivor following pre-war 'slum clearances'. It is considered to be the oldest residential house in London. The ground floor has been adapted beyond all recognition, but on the next two floors sets of protruding rectangular bay windows, made of timber and topped by pediments, are a very unusual sight. They are slightly reminiscent of the wood cabin extensions on the houses of Baltic towns like Sopot, or the teetering upper storeys in Porto's old town. Some famous visitors, including Churchill and the Queen Mother, have signed the leaded glass with a diamond pen. The strangest thing about Cloth Fair is that several of the otherwise nondescript new houses on this street mimic this bay-window feature, as if they were all star-struck infants imitating a cool elder sibling. It seems very apt that John Betjeman, whose campaigns saved several places in this book, lived next door for twenty years. The poet laureate's apartment still has his William Morris wallpaper, and is sometimes available for short-term rent.

ALDGATE

SYNAGOGUE CANDELABRA
Bevis Marks Synagogue, 4 Heneage Lane, EC3A 5DQ

Built in 1701, this is the oldest synagogue in Britain, and it is said that its Quaker architect waived his fee. With a straightforward box shape, pews and an upper gallery focusing on a Renaissance ark, it does not feel terribly different from neighbouring places of worship by Wren or

Hawksmoor. The clear glass of the broad, round-topped windows dispels any gloom that might linger in the dark wooden pews, and shows off the yellow marble pillars that prop up the gallery. The large wooden ark, painted to resemble marble, shows the ten commandments written in Hebrew; again, much like a City church. The most memorable feature is a set of seven huge, very low-hanging chandelier candelabra in brass that really dominate the space. Each one has numerous arms in the shape of sine waves and resembles a gigantic spider from some disaster movie, descending on thread. The candelabra stand for the seven days of the week and, at the centre, the largest represents the Sabbath. You cannot help but pity the poor soul whose job is to polish them. Benjamin Disraeli's family were regulars here, but following a quarrel with the synagogue his father instead had him baptized at St Andrew Holborn – allowing the boy later to become prime minister.

CROOKED WINDOWS
Hoop & Grapes, 47 Aldgate High Street, EC3N 1AL

The Hoop & Grapes pub may be half a mile away from the bobbing tide of the Thames, but if you look out of the windows too long you will be liable to go green around the gills. This sixteenth-century pub is famous for having narrowly survived the Great Fire of London, which was stopped a few yards away. Over the centuries, the timber frame has come under strain to the point that the pub leans forward by eighteen inches. The crooked building resembles a more extreme version of those old houses in Amsterdam that seem to drunkenly prop each other up, and its early Georgian sash windows slant at an angle that will play havoc with your equilibrium after a few pints. On the brink of collapse by the 1980s, the pub was restored at great expense. During this work all manner of odd antique objects were found behind the bedroom panelling, such as meat cleavers and riding crops. The toilets are located in thirteenth-century cellars, with bricked-up passages accompanied by rumours about smugglers and tunnels to the river and the Tower of London. One of the Hoop & Grapes' unique features, currently covered up, is a listening tube that allowed people in the cellar to eavesdrop on conversations upstairs. The landlord was believed to be in the pay of Oliver Cromwell, and under instruction to monitor those conspirators who got together just outside the city walls. To find the pub you need to negotiate the fiendish traffic of the four-lane gyratory system around Aldgate High St. It makes this old pub the archetypal calm in the eye of the storm.

TOWER HILL

ANCHOR OF THE *AMSTERDAM*
St Katharine Docks, 50 St Katharine's Way, E1W 1LA

Just east of Tower Bridge on the northern side are St Katharine Docks, a pretty marina where the only jarring note is struck by the brutalist Tower Hotel looming overhead. The docks' warehouses were largely destroyed in the Blitz, and the area was given the usual flats-and-restaurants makeover in the 1990s. An eighteenth-century brewery has been converted into a large pub, and the place does not feel as sterile as regenerated areas often can. Where the east basin meets the central basin, the walkway corner is occupied by a vast anchor. This belonged to the *Amsterdam*, one of the eighteenth-century cargo ships tasked with carrying money, firearms and building materials to the Dutch colonies in what is now Indonesia, and bringing back precious Javanese textiles and spices. Blighted by bad luck, the *Amsterdam* would never get this far; its first two voyages were aborted by storms in the English Channel, while a third attempt saw plague, mutiny and the sinking of the boat just past Hastings. The wreck was discovered in 1969, and its anchor brought to London. In the Hastings suburb of Bulverhythe, the ship can still be seen during low tides, the top of its ribs poking up through the sand.

MIND THE GAP
Tower Bridge, Tower Bridge Road, SE1 2UP

Tower Bridge is to London as the Eiffel Tower or Colosseum are to Paris or Rome; an instantly recognizable icon that inspires affection, and without which London wouldn't be quite the same. Like the Eiffel, it looks great in the background, especially at night. The closer you get, the less impressive it seems. The bridge opened in 1894 but impersonates a much older structure, with its slightly naff baronial look mitigated by the winged beasts hanging off its gates. That the bridge opens up is an exemplary piece of Victorian engineering, one which provided the East End with a bridge and still allowed tall-masted ships to deliver cargo to central London. One of the terrible jobs I had upon moving to London was based just south of Tower Bridge. Colleagues warned me that the bridge would open at 8.55 a.m. and 5.05 p.m. every day, and my then girlfriend hooted with laughter that I should be gullible enough to believe the bridge would be closed to traffic in rush hour. It turned out to be true. The raising of the bridge has caused a few mishaps; in 1952 it opened when a bus was halfway across. The driver saved his passengers by deciding, action-movie style, to slam his foot on the accelerator. In 1997 President Clinton, running late, was separated from his motorcade when the bridge opened. Crossing on foot, you are unlikely to encounter such dire straits, but can still experience a mild frisson of peril by looking down at the joint halfway. There is a gap, just a couple of centimetres wide, where the two parts meet. Narrow enough to be harmless, but wide enough that you can see the murky waters of the Thames bobbing beneath your feet.

HORSES
Minster Court, Mincing Lane, EC3R 7DD

Built in 1992, Minster Court is an oddly sinister hybrid at the heart of the city. Clad in peachy pink granite, it stacks up layers and layers of jagged gables and sharp triangular ends to the point where it could be an M. C. Escher drawing. The rear of the building on Mark Lane resembles a gigantic hedgehog's back. Its scale, and the echoes of Gothic in its detail, stake its claim to be a cathedral of finance. As seen from Mincing Lane, the centre of the building sits back from its two wings and financiers enter up a flight of stairs. On the plaza at the top of the stairs are three magnificent bronze horses, mid-stride. These burly beasts have been nicknamed Sterling, Dollar and Yen; if there was a lame donkey bringing up the rear it would presumably be christened Euro. Their centre-stage positioning must be a doff of the cap to San Marco in Venice, also built by a very mercantile people. Minster Court acquired a double-edged celebrity when the live-action remake of *101 Dalmatians* chose it for the headquarters of Cruella de Vil.

BLACKFRIARS

COURTYARD
The Worshipful Society of Apothecaries, Black Friars Lane, EC4V 6EJ

While wandering the City, if you should spot an outlandish coat of arms above a doorway you will most likely be in front of one of London's 110 livery companies, the descendants of our medieval guilds. Often the entrance will lead to a beautiful courtyard of porticoes and classical statues, whose quiet provides a sharp contrast to the stress-out crowds beyond. Some guilds are happy for strangers to pop their heads in for a quick look, others will sternly inform you that you are on private property. This one appears not to deny permission. Walking up Blackfriars Lane, you meet an unpromising tall building of brown bricks that looks like it might house a prison yard. Carry on and a doorway announces Apothecaries' Hall, its pediment interrupted by a strange emblem with gold unicorns, a young Apollo astride a baby dragon and a blue cat sitting on a knight's helmet. To step inside is to travel from the banks of the Thames to Tallinn Old Town; big old windows, a wooden bench, a flight of steps and a lamp at the centre. Stucco walls are painted a cool pastel yellow. There's a noticeboard advising which candidates have satisfied the examiners, a memorial tablet for the apothecary to the Georgian kings and offices including those of the Worshipful Company of Spectacle Makers, who are unlikely to offer two pairs for £69.

THE BACK BAR
The Blackfriar, 174 Queen Victoria Street, EC4V 4EG

The finest pubs in my hometown of Belfast are said to have been decorated in the years following Catholic emancipation. Italian craftsmen were brought over to install new altar-pieces, and enterprising landlords persuaded them to undertake a few jobs on the side. One wonders if a similar story lies behind this astonishing bar. A narrow wedge-shaped building facing Blackfriars Bridge, it catches the eye with gold-on-green mosaic tiles, promising 'brandies' and a 'saloon bar'. The exterior barely hints, however, at the riotous scenes within. Under a timber-beam roof is enough streaked yellow marble to make a cardinal blush. Just above head height, bronze reliefs populate the walls; jolly Rabelaisian monks busy themselves with music, viticulture and merry-making. But the crowning glory is the small room at the rear, reached through three low doorways, which feels far more like a private chapel than a place to eat scampi and chips. Myriad mirrors make up for the lack of windows and intensify the hermetic feel. Mosaic patterns decorate a round-arched roof. Demonic homunculi with books and easels perch upon marble walls lined with mottos that seem to lampoon the temperance movement ('Industry

Is All', 'Finery Is Foolery'). The pub is now run by the insipid Nicholson chain and the back room reserved for diners. As with St Pancras station, we have John Betjeman to thank for the fact that the pub avoided the wrecking ball in the 1960s.

LIST OF DESTINATIONS
Blackfriars Station, 179 Queen Victoria Street, EC4V 4EG

Just before the mainline platforms at Blackfriars, resting on the wall is a tall slab of red-brown stone into which are carved eleven rows of gold-lettered plaques. The handsome plaques offer a list of potential destinations for the traveller, and alternate towns in Kent with glamorous cities of Europe. Beckenham sits next to Baden-Baden, Faversham next to Florence, and Westgate-on-Sea next to Venice. It all looks like someone's idea of a joke. The stonework dates from 1886, when the station was known as St Paul's and run by London, Chatham & Dover Railways (LC&DR). In the decades before flight, the railways made the continent much more accessible. Providing a fast train to Dover and steamers to Boulogne or Calais, LC&DR was the Ryanair of its time. The original Blackfriars Bridge became too weak for modern trains and was dismantled in 1985. Walk to the Thames and you will see the surreal sight of its remains, four pairs of red pillars stranded in the river and looking like elephantine letterboxes. On the South Bank, two large LC&DR insignia remain where the bridge ended. For the twenty-first-century traveller, the Eurostar terminal at St Pancras brings this age back to life somewhat by offering the dual possibilities of Brussels and Lille, or Derby and Corby.

EMBANKMENT

10 ADAM STREET
WC2R 0DE

With around a hundred rooms, 10 Downing St is far bigger than it looks; however, it says something about the unassuming nature of the British that we place our head of government in a modest Georgian terrace house instead of a monumental palace. The house was originally jerry-built by an unscrupulous property speculator, and behind its famous front the building has had to be reconstructed more than once. It was given to Robert Walpole, the first prime minister, by George II but it was only in 1902 that Arthur Balfour instituted the tradition that the PM should be based here. These days, unless you are granted permission to deliver a petition, the closest you will get to 'No. 10' is the set of gates at the Whitehall end of the street. Handily, however, a near-replica exists for those who fancy playing the statesman, broadcasting speeches from its doorstep or just posing for the camera. The iron railings, the soot-blackened brick and the fan-shaped window above a slender black door can all be found at 10 Adam St, a quiet turning off the Strand obscured by a large gym. The door number is in gold rather than white and the overhead lamp is missing, but this doppelgänger will fool all except the most attentive. It was used for Meryl Streep's Thatcher biopic *The Iron Lady*. At the time of writing, No. 9 is a large building site, so you may get a few stares from the workmen as you promise 'peace in our time'.

YORK WATERGATE
Watergate Walk, WC2N 6DU

The Embankment as we know it was designed by Joseph Bazalgette and reclaimed a stretch of marshland. In the seventeenth century the area behind Embankment Gardens was lined with riverside mansions, desirable for their direct access to the transport possibilities of the Thames. One such mansion was York House, whose last owner was George Villiers, Duke of Buckingham. When the land was bought by developers and the house demolished, his condition was that the five new streets should take his name and title (right down to 'Of Alley', now York Place). The only reminder of these grand houses is York Watergate at the northern edge of the gardens, now stranded over 100 metres from the river. Attributed by some to Inigo Jones, it is a very handsome structure and causes a tinge of regret that the main house is no more. Based on the Medici fountain in Paris, it contains three arches; two small side arches offer shelter to anyone waiting for a boat, and a central arch has a flight of steps that would have led into the water. The stone is rusticated, and matched by two weatherworn lions above. When the streets were laid out, Samuel Pepys moved into Buckingham St and would have used this gate to access the Thames. With sea levels projected to keep rising, perhaps it could yet become a gateway to the river once more.

ANGLO–BELGIAN MEMORIAL
Victoria Embankment, WC2N

In 1914 Britain went to war, and nothing was ever quite the same again. Millions of Britons fought and laid down their lives to defend the freedom of a nation. That nation was Belgium. Many had hoped that Britain could sit out the mutual devastation of World War I, until Germany violated a treaty with their invasion of the neutral Belgians. Some 250,000 Belgian refugees were taken in by Britain and a temporary village outside Gateshead, Elisabethsville, was run as a Belgian enclave using Belgian currency. The Belgians were swiftly and unceremoniously repatriated after the war, but left some oblique traces. Agatha Christie's contact with Belgians in Devon inspired her to create Hercule Poirot, and some Sheffield butchers were still selling horse meat in the 1970s. A more substantial reminder is found on Victoria Embankment in the form of a memorial 'to the British nation, from the grateful people of Belgium'. Inside a broad curved wall of Portland stone, flanked by allegorical figures of Justice and Honour, stands a plinth with three sleek bronze figures. A mournful woman, presumably Belgium herself, is pointing westwards to a nude boy and girl, their modesty kept intact by the stacks of wreaths and garlands they are carrying. The image of fatherless, penniless children being sent away to safety is a poignant one. The monument was unveiled in 1920, and three years later Britain reciprocated with a memorial in Brussels that marks the help given to British prisoners and casualties.

CLEOPATRA'S NEEDLE
Victoria Embankment, WC2N

When the Romans conquered Egypt, they carried back obelisks as trophies and eight Egyptian obelisks can be found there today, in such key sites as St Peter's Square and Piazza del Popolo. Wishing to emulate the empire of the Caesars, London, New York and Paris have their own Egyptian obelisks. All three share the gauche misnomer of Cleopatra's Needle, despite preceding the famous queen by more than a millennium. London's needle dates to around 1450 BC and the reign of Thutmose III, with some hieroglyphs added 200 years later to mark the victories of Rameses II. During the reign of the Roman emperor Augustus, the steeple was moved from Heliopolis to a temple at Alexandria. At some point it was toppled and lay buried in the sands, preserving the hieroglyphs. Excavated by the Italian adventurer Giovanni Battista Belzoni, in 1819 it was presented to Britain for its role in ending Napoleon's occupation of Egypt. The obelisk weighed 224 tons, so the British were reluctant to undertake the logistical nightmare of shipping it home and the gift remained in Alexandria until 1877. Five years later, ironically, Egypt would become British territory. Its transit was fraught with problems, six men dying when its bespoke vessel capsized in the Bay of Biscay. Cleopatra's Needle now stands watch over the Thames, faced by a pair of smiling bronze sphinxes. Large plaques on its plinth paraphrase the hieroglyphics and tell the history of the obelisk in appropriately Ozymandian language: 'This obelisk, prostrate for centuries upon the sands of Alexandria . . .'

SEWER LAMP
Carting Lane, WC2R

To turn off the Strand around the Savoy Hotel can make for an intriguing detour. The bowels of this august institution feel like a miniature city-state in their own right. The streets are named Savoy St, Savoy Place, Savoy Hill, Savoy Row and Savoy Way. Most of the time you will be alone with the hotel staff as they receive deliveries, push around vast trolleys of laundry or savour a quick cigarette. Hiding among these tall buildings and narrow alleyways are the private chapel of the Queen and London's last remaining sewer gas lamp. These lamps were popular in the Victorian era; they provided lighting while burning off the noxious gases in London's sewerage. Domes in the sewer roof collected methane, which was then diverted into hollow lampposts. The story is a popular one, as people are amused by the notion of the streets of London being lit up by the waste matter of the Savoy's distinguished guests. In truth, the lamps were powered by the mains gas supply, and the burning of the sewer gas was simply a means to remove impurities from the air. The lamp had to be restored a few years ago after being felled by a reversing lorry. Those who loiter around Carting Lane still report a distinct whiff of cabbage.

District Line

I moved to London just long enough ago to remember when the District line's carriages had wooden floors, as pictured on Blur's *Modern Life is Rubbish* sleeve. Today its carriages have been modernized. In the nineteenth century, train providers were eager to extend their services into outer London because it was much cheaper than drilling under the centre to complete the Circle line and paying compensation to the people affected. For a time in the nineteenth century, the line ran to locations as distant as Windsor and Southend. The line has numerous branches in the west, covering the idyllic spots of Richmond, Wimbledon and Kew, which meet up at Earl's Court before running along the Thames, into the traditional East End and on into the new East End areas of Barking and Dagenham. Earl's Court was the site of the first Underground escalator, which in 1911 connected the District and Piccadilly lines. There are a few heritage maps and signs dotted across the District line's stations; look out for the stencilled 'To the Trains' notice at Stepney Green.

WEST HAM

ABBEY MILLS PUMPING STATION
Abbey Lane, E15 2RW

Today, dirty work is hidden behind a screen (probably advertising luxury goods), 'out of sight and out of mind' being the principle. Few are prepared to tackle the messy, necessary jobs under our streets. The Victorians allotted a bit more dignity to those whose labour kept London running. Joseph Bazalgette, creator of our sewer system, tackled the Great Stink of the mid-nineteenth century like an evangelical preacher out to save souls. One of his pumping stations, sitting in the long grasses beyond the East End where the Lea River meets Bow Creek, has come to be known as 'The Cathedral of Sewage'. The shape is cruciform; above the roof is a polygonal dome, which looks oddly Russian Orthodox, surrounded by four small stone turrets. Below these, each window is housed within a striped Romanesque arch. The design helps itself to elements from Byzantine, Moorish and Venetian architecture, in the process coming off as Kazan-meets-Cordoba. The point is to sanctify the work going on within. The best view of the station is to turn off Stratford High St along Greenway. Continuing to operate as a back-up, it is rigorously fenced off from the public. Early birds who book the few available appointments during the annual Open House weekend can enjoy the equally decorative ironwork within.

MONUMENT

MICE AND CHEESE
23 Eastcheap, EC3M 1DE

It takes an eagle eye to spot this sculpture, as diminutive, discreet and delightful as any in London. On the corner of Eastcheap and Philpot Lane stands a vaguely Italianate building painted cream, pink and light blue, currently home to a coffee chain. Look along the ledge, and at the rear corner you will spot two life-size brown mice, burrowing into either end of what looks like a lump of cheddar. There are various implausible explanations for their provenance. The most recurrent is that they are a memorial to two labourers on Wren's Monument, sited around the corner. The workmen fell to their deaths while brawling over a vanished cheese sandwich, which it transpired had been eaten by mice. Less credible still is the myth that a London merchant loaned Dick Whittington's cat to a king in Asia, and was richly rewarded when it killed all his mice. Originally a spice merchant's offices, the building did not arrive on Eastcheap until 1862, suggesting that the Monument hypothesis caught on simply because it was a good story. Should you find yourself forced to come to blows with a colleague at work (we've all been there), it's best not to do so at the summit of a 200-foot column.

CAMELS
Peek House, 20 Eastcheap, EC3M 1EB

Directly across the road from the mice and cheese (see above), the corner of Eastcheap and Lovat Lane offers a glimpse of the Sahara Desert, as unlikely as it is romantic.

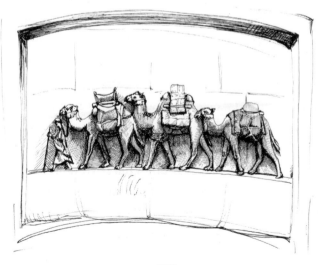

Above the doorway of an uninspiring retail outlet, a robed Arab clutches his walking staff and leads a train of three camels, burdened with boxes and bags of goods. In the foreground is a skeletal ribcage. The original occupants of this 1883 building were Peek Bros, importers of tea, coffee and spices, including a 'Camel' tea brand. The sculptor was William Theed the Younger, who had cornered the market in camels, having already delivered one for the Africa section of the Albert Memorial. The company ceased trading in 1958, condemning the camels to carry their wares across the sandy slopes ever since. Passing financiers in receipt of a seven-figure bonus may care to note that the eye of the needle is not pictured.

ISAAC MILNER MEMORIAL
St Mary-at-Hill Church, Lovat Lane, EC3R 8EE

Most of us have at some point wondered what will be etched on our gravestone when the time comes. A friend of mine is considering 'Here lies [name]. Serves him right.' Faced with the final curtain, others take refuge in verbosity. A Wren church heavily restored after a fire in 1988, St Mary-at-Hill can be found tucked away on Lovat Lane. Its elegant white space is today denuded of pews and chiefly used as a concert venue. People admire the interior and the well-concealed churchyard, but a highlight is one of the memorial graves in the corner of the foyer. Isaac Milner (d. 1713) was evidently quite a man, or so he wants to tell us. His coat of arms interrupts a pediment over two columns, flanked by cherubim standing on skulls and drying their eyes with handkerchiefs. Starring role goes to an inscription of some fifty-six lines, an additional slab having had to be added beneath. We learn the names of his wife and ten children, the burial sites of those who did not survive him, the various social groups who mourn him, his personal qualities (including his conversational skills), his values and attitudes, how he lived his life, and those relatives who followed him into the tomb along with all relevant dates and ages. This text makes Polonius look taciturn; just when it seems to be winding down and reaching its conclusion, it bursts back to life with new topics on which to pontificate. Whenever I read it, I hear the voice of Michael Palin as some blithe Pythonesque vicar.

LONDON STONE
111 Cannon Street, EC4N 5AR

The tourist attractions of one age can plummet into obscurity in another. Google 'London Stone' today and the first two results are a theme pub and a paving company, yet in previous centuries London Stone was a chief city landmark and rivalled Charing Cross as the exact centre of London. The chunk of limestone was said to be Roman, or druidical, to have contained Excalibur, or to have been brought to London by Trojan refugees. More credible hypotheses connect it to the Roman governor's palace or

King Alfred's ninth-century street plan. No one knows the origins of London Stone, but the earliest written reference, a list of Canterbury Cathedral's London holdings, has been dated to around 1100. In *Henry VI Part 2*, Shakespeare has the Kentish rebel Jack Cade use London Stone as a throne when he seizes the city. The stone was damaged in the Great Fire of 1666, and one story has Elizabeth I's astrologer John Dee removing segments for its purported magical properties. What remains of the stone today is half a metre wide. In 1742 the stone was attached to St Swithin's Church. The church was destroyed in the Blitz, and now no one seems keen to find it a proper home. Today it lurks behind a grubby sheet of scuffed Perspex, on ground level, beneath WHSmith promotions for a meal deal. Next time you pass 111 Cannon St, look upon the fizzy-drink posters and despair.

TEMPLE

CRUSADER KNIGHTS
Temple Church, EC4Y 7BB

It's no surprise that Temple Church makes an appearance in *The Da Vinci Code*. Consecrated in 1185, this was the venue for initiation ceremonies into the Knights Templar. The oldest section, the round church at the west end, was modelled on Jerusalem's Church of the Holy Sepulchre. Its stout rotunda shape and round-arched doorway evoke early Christianity, but after post-Blitz restoration much of the church does not look its age; one could mistake it all for a nineteenth-century flight of fancy. The spiral staircase to the upper floor is convincingly Norman, and grail-hunters will thrill at the effigies of ten crusader knights laid across the floor, marking their burial here. Innocent-looking Romanesque faces peer out through their chainmail, while other heavily eroded figures bring Pompeii to mind. Some hands are held in prayer; some hold unsheathed swords, as if they expect to leap up and resume battle on the Day of Judgement. Not that the scene is sombre or foreboding. The church is bathed in light and a diverse array of gurning, cackling gargoyle faces line the walls, looking like theatre masks from ancient Athens. They give this old place a peculiar levity.

ROMANIAN ICONOSTASIS
St Dunstan-in-the-West, 186a Fleet Street, EC4A 2HR

Although this church was constructed in 1832, there has been one on its Fleet St site for almost a millennium. It seems appropriate, therefore, that St Dunstan's should be a partial composite of older features from other places. Anyone walking down Fleet St may have noticed the giants behind the church's clock face, whose clubs strike the bells, or the statue of Elizabeth I, sculpted in her own lifetime, which originally stood over Ludgate. The distinctive octagonal spire is a preview of the church's interior, itself eight-sided with broad, shallow chapels of equal size underneath a celestial vaulted ceiling in Giotto blue. The church is currently shared between Anglicans and the Romanian Orthodox Church, and it is interesting to see busts, memorial tablets and Gothic carvings sitting next to luridly coloured paintings in the Byzantine style. To the left of the altar, taking up one of the recesses, is a vast wooden iconostasis, transported from Antim Monastery in Bucharest. The paintings inside are rather faded, but in any case play second fiddle to the intricate patterns framing them. A crucifix is posed above a crown spire, with lamps on either side. From the centre emerges a four-poster canopy resembling a throne, which contains a holy book on a marble lectern. It is a surprise to enter from Fleet St and be met by an echo of the famous wooden churches of Maramureş.

CHINAMEN
Twinings Museum, 216 Strand, WC2R 1AP

One could easily miss the diminutive, narrow façade of Twinings' headquarters, nestled between the lofty showpieces where Fleet St meets the Strand. Twinings has been trading tea from this site since 1706, a few decades after coffee houses had been established as the Twitter of their day. The Strand premises were the first tearooms in

Britain, Chinese tea having been introduced as a luxury item by Charles II's Portuguese wife. As the fiefdoms of the East India Company spread, so did the tea-drinking habit. By the nineteenth century the rites of tea were cemented at the centre of the British psyche, where they remain today. Some have argued that without the health benefits of forsaking gin and ale for tea, the Industrial Revolution might not have been possible. Above two Corinthian columns, a simple pediment contains the centuries-old logo, a golden lion (the original name of Thomas Twining's establishment) and two reclining Chinese chaps in traditional costume, looking like Hergé's Thompson twins in one of their less convincing disguises. One wears a fetching blue tunic, the other a wide-brimmed hat and what strangely resembles leopardskin. The orientalism of these figures might be dated and redundant today, but it adds a welcome splash of colour to the streetscape.

'ROMAN' BATH
5 Strand Lane, WC2R 1AP

Hunting for the Roman bath is significantly more fun than finding it. Just behind St Mary le Strand, walk towards the river down quiet Surrey St. On your right-hand side is an entrance to the defunct Aldwych Underground station, which ceased to function in 1994 and now chiefly serves as a film location. Further down on the same side is a long row of buildings in orange brick and pale terracotta, with

Roman-style gurning faces around the doorways. In the middle of this terrace is a low arch to a gated alleyway, with an ancient-looking sign from the National Trust advertising the Roman bath. The tunnel ends with a steep flight of steps that takes you to the minute cul-de-sac of Strand Lane. Look right, and in one corner are some iron railings. Step inside and the window looks down into the bath: an external light switch illuminates the interior. The bath itself, truth be told, is a bit of an anti-climax – certainly no Pompeiian frescoes or mosaics. A sign on the railings tells its history and admits that the bath is unlikely to be Roman at all. It's situated a mile outside the boundaries of Roman London, and historians think the bath was probably installed in the early seventeenth century, perhaps as a reservoir, when the 2nd Earl of Arundel had his house here. First mention of the bath comes in 1784 but by the nineteenth century it is being trumpeted as Roman. This implies that someone saw the vaguely Roman brickwork, put two and two together, and came up with a five-star marketing ploy. On a few days each year the public are admitted inside for a closer look, but appointments must be booked a week ahead.

SLOANE SQUARE

WESTBOURNE RIVER
Sloane Square Station, SW1W 8BB

If you find yourself on the platforms at Sloane Square, look for a diagonal Tube within metal girders that passes narrowly over the trains and disappears into the arched wall opposite. This pipe contains a river, flowing above your head. The Thames has several tributaries in London that were covered over as the capital sprawled outwards. These are generally no longer visible, but their names have left a trace. The largest, the Fleet, was a major river in Roman London and gave its name to Fleet St. The Tyburn did the same for the notorious execution site the Tyburn Tree; Oxford St and Park Lane were originally named after it. The Westbourne river rises at Hampstead and, via Kilburn, Bayswater and Knightsbridge, joins the Thames at Chelsea. The Serpentine in Hyde Park was created by building a dam across the Westbourne. Used for drinking water in previous centuries, the Industrial Revolution rendered the Westbourne an open sewer and, when the neighbourhoods of west London were laid out, it became subterranean. In the first half of the nineteenth century the river was directed into pipes, one of which can be seen cutting through Sloane Square station. The Westbourne is close to the end of its course here, meeting the Thames between Chelsea Bridge and the Royal Hospital. For an illustration of how London's lost subterranean rivers can grip the imagination, read Ben Aaronovitch's amusing fantasy/police procedural hybrid *Rivers of London*, in which colourful personifications of the rivers appear as a supporting cast.

THE PHEASANTRY
152 King's Road, SW3 4UT

The King's Rd has adopted many guises over the years, few of them as culturally barren as the current reign of Sloane Rangers and oligarchs. Charles II travelled to Kew this way, and it remained a private road until 1830. In the twentieth century it was a hotbed of activity. Mosley's blackshirts had a barracks here and it was the epicentre of mod and punk cultures in the sixties and seventies. Britain's first Starbucks opened on the King's Rd, and chain stores have since hollowed out the place where things used to happen. The Chelsea Drugstore of *A Clockwork Orange* fame is now a McDonald's, and the Pheasantry catches the eye in spite of housing Pizza Express. Its bright-red brick façade sits back from the road behind a low balustraded wall and a round archway propped up by two caryatids. Between them is a roundel with a fresco of a couple, presumably Charles II and Nell Gwynn. On top of the arch, a little charioteer drives four galloping horses. There is a blue plaque for the Princess Serafina Astafieva, great niece to Tolstoy, who ran a ballet school here. There are also three plaques advertising the services of a decorator, upholsterer and cabinet maker. This jumble suggests an interesting backstory and the Pheasantry does not disappoint. Originally the premises of a pheasant breeder, the decorators, the Jouberts, took over in the 1880s and added that eccentric miniature *arc de triomphe*. The last Joubert retiring in 1932, for thirty years the Pheasantry was a club for artists and actors, frequented by Francis Bacon, Dylan Thomas and other notable drunkards. The house then became apartments with a basement nightclub, with Lou Reed, Sparks and Queen playing here on their way up. Eric Clapton lived upstairs in what was by all accounts a fairly bohemian set-up; one incident involved a dyed-green rabbit jumping off the roof after being given LSD. By that point the building was deteriorating and only the efforts of John Betjeman prevented its demolition. Perhaps Pizza Express and McDonald's are the price we must pay for preservation.

ATALANTA
Albert Bridge Gardens, Chelsea Embankment, SW3

Facing onto the Thames and Battersea Park, Cheyne Walk has long been one of London's most exclusive addresses. Its eighteenth-century houses have attracted the likes of Lloyd George, Whistler, Turner, the Rolling Stones and George Best. People have not been put off by the creation of the Embankment, whose incessant traffic now separates the houses from the river. An artistic centre in its heyday, its gardens are home to numerous sculptures, with Sir Thomas More, Carlyle and Rossetti all represented. The most famous of these is David Wynne's cloying boy swimming with a dolphin. Just after Albert Bridge is a bronze cast of *Atalanta*, the only female Argonaut, by Francis Derwent Wood. A candid nude with her hair tied up, she faces us but turns her head away, prefiguring Modigliani's women. Stood by a tree stump, Atalanta is supposed to be preparing for her mythical race with Hippomenes, but the pose is as unceremonious as if she had just stepped out of the bath. Doubtless the statue was positioned here to look onto the Thames, but she now appears to be averting her gaze from horrid apartment blocks and glass buildings across the river (which include Norman Foster's practice). Wood, who opened a clinic to sculpt and paint thin copper masks for soldiers disfigured in World War I, also made the controversial Machine Gun Corps memorial that stands at Hyde Park Corner.

YOUNG MOZART
Orange Square, Pimlico Road, SW1W 8NE

The music of Mozart feels particularly pure, because that effortless virtuosity is never delivered with a sneer. It is put at the service of smiling, vivacious, and very human sentiments. Like a pink sunset or a good cognac, it is one of those compensations for being alive that makes the whole wretched business seem worth it. Mozart is more readily associated with Salzburg or Vienna, but he did spend just over a year in London, part of the child prodigy's Grand Tour through the courts of northern Europe. He was well received, performing three times for George III and fascinating the scientific community. The Mozarts initially rented a home on Cecil Court, but when father Leopold fell ill they moved to Chelsea, still outside London at the time, at 180 Ebury St. This was where a bored and housebound eight-year-old Mozart completed his first symphony before the family moved to 20 Frith St. A few yards from the Mozarts' home, Ebury St ends with Orange Square, an attractive triangular space with greenery, benches and a posh French restaurant. There is a 1994 bronze of the young, grinning Mozart, smartly dressed with violin resting on his shoulder. Pages of notation lie at his feet as if just dashed off. The boy wonder boosts his height by standing on two hefty hardback volumes of sheet music, as if he were hoping for a kiss from the ladies for whom he is playing. Mozart's first symphony is (whisper it) not actually that good, but there were forty more to come, and the early start laid the foundations for many a masterpiece.

FARNESE HERCULES
Ormonde Place, SW1W 8HX

No visit to Naples would be complete without a tour of the Archaeological Museum, which holds the finest treasures of Pompeii and Herculaneum. The spine of the museum is provided by the Farnese collection, which Pope Paul III acquired as the remains of classical Rome were being excavated. One of its most celebrated pieces is a ten-foot marble statue of Hercules at rest. The Farnese version is a copy of the lost original by Alexander the Great's sculptor Lysippos. There are a few copies of the *Farnese Hercules* in circulation and happily London has one in the open air – if you know where to look. Turn off Orange Square at Bourne St. The first left turn is down Bunhouse Place, an alleyway behind Pimlico Rd, which leads to Ormonde Place, a leafy and secluded neo-Georgian square. Hercules takes centre-stage. His rippling muscles and colossal limbs mark him out as an extraordinary specimen of a man, yet he is plainly exhausted after his labours, staring blankly downwards and leaning on his club, which is draped in a lion skin. The Ormonde Place copy has been scaled down and does lose something in the process, but its presence in an obscure residential corner shows how much money there is in Belgravia.

HAMMERSMITH

THE WORLD'S SMALLEST BAR ROOM
The Dove, 19 Upper Mall, W6 9TA

West of Hammersmith Bridge, the Thames starts to feel properly bucolic and a long way from the commotion of central London. On Lower Mall, pleasant pubs face the river; the opposite bank is thick with trees and a community of moored houseboats is accessed by wooden piers. It could as easily be Oxfordshire as London W6. The most historic of these pubs is the Dove, accessed through the passage leading from the gardens to Upper Mall. It was here that James Thomson wrote the lyrics for 'Rule, Britannia!'; the pub asserts that Charles II wined and dined Nell Gwynn here, all the more impressive since it was built after his death in 1685. The riverside terrace is a pleasant place to sit, but the feature that put this eighteenth-century pub into *The Guinness Book of Records* dates from around 1910. To the right of the bar is the world's smallest bar room, measuring four-foot-two by seven-foot-ten. Pubs needed a separate saloon bar to qualify for a full licence to sell both beer and spirits. Applying to the strict magistrates for permission to make structural alterations was a risky business, so the Dove simply installed one clandestinely at the dead of night and presented the bar as a fait accompli. One nearby sight of note is the house of William Morris, giant of the Arts and Crafts movement. A few doors from the Dove, it features a gilded engraving with a few lines from his *News from Nowhere*.

PUTNEY BRIDGE

WILLIAM POWELL ALMSHOUSES
Church Gate, SW6 3LB

At the Fulham end of Putney Bridge, pass through the back gate of All Saints' Churchyard. The church is famous for an appearance in *The Omen*, in which Patrick Troughton's eccentric priest is killed by lightning. To your left, behind a low gate you will notice a long and narrow garden lined by roses, and surrounded by an L-shaped terrace of striking neo-medieval houses. This secluded spot is the William Powell almshouses, a dozen small flats that to this day are kept for elderly women. The original seventeenth-century houses were rebuilt by the Victorians, who went to town on loud decorative motifs. The stone and brick used is a warm, sandy colour. Facing the street, the houses announce themselves with carvings of six women standing in niches, each captured in a pious pose. Above them are the garlanded faces of three graces: Faith, Hope and Charity. The two-floor flats themselves are all pointed arches. A tiled loggia roof runs along the façade, under which Gothic bay windows, with tiny rose windows between their points, alternate with sheltered doorways. Even the drainpipes end in sculptures of large, gasping fish. The time when the poor were considered worthy of such top-notch craftsmanship seems increasingly distant.

PAVILION
Craven Cottage, Stevenage Road, SW6 6HH

Many of England's football clubs have either redeveloped their original Archibald Leitch stadia beyond recognition, or abandoned them altogether for soulless domes in business parks miles from the town centre. Fulham FC having never quite struck the big time, their venerable old Craven Cottage ground has come through the decades relatively unscathed. The site has history; built on Anne Boleyn's hunting grounds, the original cottage was the home of author Edward Bulwer-Lytton (coiner of such enduring phrases as 'the great unwashed' and 'it was a dark and stormy night'), the sportsmen moving in after it burnt down in 1888. On the banks of the Thames and with the Bishop of London's medieval palace for a next-door neighbour, it is an unusually pastoral location for a football ground. You expect to find cricket here, and the sensation is amplified when you pass through the fancy gable-topped turnstiles and see a small pavilion in the corner between two stands. This unique feature contains some VIP seating on its upper balcony, as well as the changing rooms. The manager's dugout is on the opposite side of the pitch, giving personnel a rather awkward walk across the pitch when they might prefer to vanish down an adjacent tunnel. In an age when football is packaged as a slick Hollywood product, this is charming. The good people of my beloved Millwall would not shirk this opportunity to pelt underperformers or opponents with coins; however, the genteel locale has rubbed off on Fulham fans, who are less visceral and partisan than the norm. A section of the ground is designated for 'neutral' supporters, a thing unheard of elsewhere.

TURNHAM GREEN

IONIC TEMPLE
Chiswick House and Gardens, Burlington Lane, W4 2RP

Nature is not cuddly or benign. It is harsh and indifferent. Allow wilderness to take over and you will have scrub, thickets and thorns; a walk from A to B is

more likely to leave you with sprains and cuts than an appreciation of untarnished beauty. It is surprising that the early landscape gardeners of England believed their creations to be reflective of nature; they were wonderful precisely because they were man-made. Chiswick House was built by Richard Boyle, 3rd Earl of Burlington, known by his contemporaries as 'the architect Earl'. As a young man, Burlington became smitten with Andrea Palladio's take on Vitruvian architecture and his enthusiasm led to it becoming a signature of the eighteenth century. With more than a passing resemblance to Palladio's La Rotonda in Vicenza, Chiswick House was an attempt to create an authentic Roman villa, with linked chambers around a central hall, octagonal like the large dome above it. The gardens are free to enter and not to be missed if you have a taste for the classical world. One jewel is the Ionic Temple. With a triangular pediment, a portico and a dome roof, it resembles a toytown Pantheon. The gardens around it slope downwards like an amphitheatre towards the pond at the centre. Emerging from the waters is a plinth with an obelisk, reinforcing the Pantheon resemblance. If wealth is to be distributed so unequally in this world, as it appears it must, it may as well go to someone with enough good taste to leave behind treasures like Chiswick House.

GUNNERSBURY

ONION DOME
Russian Orthodox Church, 57 Harvard Road, W4 4ED

Wedged between the train tracks and the start of the M4, Harvard Rd seems an unremarkable street in Chiswick, until its chestnut trees part to reveal a church that is very un-Western in appearance. High up on its tall, whitewashed walls are minuscule windows. Its shape is complex, with square becoming cruciform as aisles rise above the four corner bays. Above the entrance porch, a belfry resembling those on Greek monasteries. The various segments of the building, all at different heights, have overhanging wooden eaves. On top of it all, a small tower is capped by a big bright blue onion dome, flecked with gold stars, and a triple-barred Orthodox cross rising from its centre. Opened in 1999, this is the British base of the self-governed Russian Orthodox Church Outside Russia or, to give it its full title, the Cathedral of the Dormition of the Most Holy Mother of God and Holy Royal Martyrs. Although designated a cathedral, its size is closer to that of a normal parish church. The walls of the church are low on ornamentation but the very colourful bulb of the dome, especially if spotted from the elevated M4, seems as unlikely as an alien spacecraft. Focus on the dome and you might be able to imagine yourself in a faraway land, and the church's walls to be coated in Siberian snow. Inside the church are various icons and relics from Russia, including a trenchcoat believed to have belonged to Tsar Nicholas II.

KEW GARDENS

MAIDS OF HONOUR
Newens, 288 Kew Road, TW9 3DU

This is the only entry dedicated to a foodstuff, but it is one with a fairly heavyweight history. A maid of honour is a sweet made of cheese curd with puff pastry casing; the official recipe is top secret but I suspect it may include ground almonds. The story told is that, one day, Henry VIII found Anne Boleyn and her attendant maids of honour scoffing these treats from a silver dish. He liked them so much that he confiscated the recipe and kept it under lock and key at Richmond Palace. One variant on the legend has him imprisoning the cook and obliging her to churn out the cakes for the rest of her life, which might have made decapitation seem a blessing. With the cakes a fixture in the royal household, word got out and by the eighteenth century a Maids of Honour bakery was doing business in Richmond. Robert Newens served an apprenticeship there, later opening his own shop. His son moved the business to 288 Kew Rd in 1850 and it has been there ever since (with maids of honour still made by hand every day), although the twee mock-Tudor building is a century younger, the Blitz having done for the original. Near Kew Gardens' entrance gates, it remains a popular destination for a retro afternoon tea surrounded by chintz, elderly ladies and *Daily Telegraph* readers in tweed.

WIMBLEDON

HAILE SELASSIE
Cannizaro Park, SW19 4UE

In a world where people worship the likes of John Terry or Russell Brand as divinities, the Rastafarian position of maintaining that Haile Selassie, Emperor of Ethiopia, is the Messiah could be considered eminently sensible. Haile Selassie himself carefully sat on the fence regarding his godhead, from which we can infer that he was quite pleased with the idea. But what has all this to do with the Wombles of Wimbledon Common? Our catalyst, to confuse matters further, is Benito Mussolini. Wishing to build a new Roman Empire and join those European states with a colonial 'place in the sun', Il Duce sent troops to conquer Ethiopia in 1935 and Haile Selassie lived out five years of exile in Britain. The Ethiopian premier bought a house in Bath, but initially lived in leafy Wimbledon. His host here, Hilda Seligman, dabbled in sculpture and had Selassie model for a bust. The bust now resides in Cannizaro Park on Wimbledon Common, hidden behind a hotel on a secluded lawn. The man himself wears a Nehru collar, clutches a scroll and strikes a quietly statesmanlike pose. His beard has a light coating of moss. If not exactly Canova working with Carrara marble, it is nonetheless a dignified bust. Cannizaro Park itself deserves to be better known; its lush gardens contain a great diversity of flora. Other sculptures include a teapot fountain with multiple spouts, and a statue of Diana cradling the head of a wounded fawn.

BUDDHAS
Buddhapadipa Temple, 14 Calonne Road, SW19 5HJ

Even by the standards of south-west London, Wimbledon Village is a chic and cloistered area, up a steep hill from the Broadway and station. Here you will find huge detached houses, and women with sunglasses and silk headscarves driving open-top cars. If you wish to attain purity by freeing yourself from desire, the best starting point might be already having enough money to live around here. On Calonne Rd there is a stunning Buddhist temple built in the Thai style, with resident nuns and monks in orange robes. Its walls and perimeter balustrade are white, with three layers of red triangular roofing over each segment. Hanging on the eaves are elaborate pieces of curling gold that frame the pediments. In the pediments and around the window frames, a background of red jewels is decorated by golden tongues of flame. The steps are guarded by two pairs of fierce oriental lions in stone and bronze, with claws and teeth bared. The interior is just as fascinating, with walls daubed with colourful frescoes showing scenes from the life of the Buddha. The depictions of Chaos and Enlightenment could be a Last Judgement in a Renaissance church. At the centre of the altar are three Buddhas in bronze, gold and emerald. The golden one was a present to Queen Elizabeth II, who regifted it to the temple upon its opening in 1982. The others are replicas of important statues from Thailand. Today the pubs of England are indissolubly wedded to Thai food, so it is quite proper that the chefs behind our new favourite cuisine should have a fine place to practise their religion. Novak Djokovic comes here to meditate during the high-pressure fortnight of the tennis championship. You are permitted to visit the grounds, provided you behave yourself. Take off your shoes before entering the temple.

RICHMOND

TOMB OF SIR RICHARD BURTON
St Mary Magdalene's RC Church, North Worple Way, SW14 8PR

Sir Richard Burton (the explorer and diplomat, not the boozy Welsh thespian) was a man with an insatiable

appetite for travel, adventure, sex and drugs. Highlights of his achievements include unexpurgated translations of the *Arabian Nights* and the *Kama Sutra*, surviving a spear through the head in Somalia, and managing to enter Mecca in cunning disguise (he stained his skin with walnut juice). His lust for life was out of step with the mores of Victorian England, and it seems apt that his exotic tomb should be an equally incongruous presence in the sleepy suburb of Mortlake. Up against a wall in the churchyard, surrounded by modest terraced houses, is a life-size imitation of a square desert tent in marble and stone with realistic draping. The cornice of the roof includes both a crucifix statue and a rather Islamic pattern of gilded crescents and stars. The biggest surprise is at the rear of the tomb, where an external stepladder leads to a pane of glass through which you can see the coffins of Burton and his wife Isabel, plus an assortment of religious effigies and Arabic jars and lanterns. Touchingly, the glass is said to have been added because Burton was afraid of the dark. The tomb's eclectic bent is an illustration of the compromise required by a devout Catholic woman and a husband who concluded that 'man never worshipped anything but himself'.

HORACE WALPOLE'S DOGS
Strawberry Hill House, 268 Waldegrave Road, TW1 4ST

Horace Walpole, son of Prime Minister Robert Walpole, was an eccentric character whose whims and visions paved the way for the Gothic revival. Walpole followed his father into Parliament on the side of the Whigs, but his lasting legacy is a strange novel, 1764's *The Castle of Otranto*, which begins with a hero being crushed to death by a gigantic helmet that has fallen from the sky. This sounds rather silly, but the book's ability to tap into irrational, subconscious fears made it highly influential: it is regarded as the first Gothic novel and the progenitor of Bram Stoker and Edgar Allan Poe. Walpole left an architectural counterpart to his novel at Strawberry Hill, just where the Thames passes Twickenham. Gothic would become the signature style of the Victorians, but in the eighteenth century Palladianism still ruled and Walpole was ahead of the curve. To look at his house is to see the advent of Romanticism, with Gothic rising from its slumber in reaction to the measured rationalism of the Enlightenment. Its eastern ogee windows are slightly Venetian and its roof is lined with battlements.

The whole is coated in gleaming white limestone stucco, which enhances the sense that you are witnessing an apparition. There is a conical turret, a round tower and little Elizabethan pot-spires at every corner. An endearing touch is the choice of statues for the entrance gates: not eagles, lions or griffins but tiny lapdogs. They stand to attention, propping up a crest with the initial W, as if expecting their master's return. The house was Walpole's great hobby horse and he would add new components over the decades. Even in Walpole's lifetime the house was a great visitor attraction, to the point where he would ask his housekeeper to conduct tours while he hid in the garden cottage.

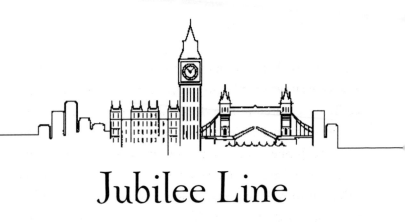

Jubilee Line

A comparative newcomer with swish trains and stations to match, this line opened in 1979 (two years after the Queen's jubilee, hence its name and silver colour) but is London's third-busiest. A Jubilee line station always has the air of a blockbuster film set about it. Canary Wharf's wide escalators to street level are particularly dramatic but Westminster, with its seventeen escalators, giant exposed concrete beams and views onto multiple floors, is the showstopper. This was planned as the Fleet line and intended to run underneath Fleet St, but all stations east of Charing Cross were scrapped. Look out for the pleasing illuminated Underground roundels on the escalators at St John's Wood: 'Way Out' on the way up, 'To Trains' on the way down. The platforms on stations dating to the 1999 extension, starting with Westminster, enjoy the innovation of suicide-proof glass walls, whose doors open in concert with the doors of trains. I do not doubt that these walls have saved many a life; as I write, today's news headlines featured a man decapitated by a Tube train on another line when he leaned forward to retrieve a dropped bag. The Jubilee line is cited by inequality campaigners as the line where life expectancy decreases by two years with each stop. It snakes through diverse parts of London from the north-west, the West End, and down to the Thames. South-east London is covered before it turns north again towards the Docklands and finishes up in Stratford. Interesting features are the 'secret cinema' at Canary Wharf and Canning Town's memorial to the men of Thames Iron Works.

ST JOHN'S WOOD

HELMET HOUSE
12 Langford Place, NW8 0LL

Horace Walpole's deadly giant helmet (see the entry on Strawberry Hill on page 184) seems a little less risible when you visit Langford Place, and find yourself face to face with a huge helmet shape that, were it to fall from the sky, might not be guaranteed to flatten a man but would at least leave him severely maimed. The 'helmet' is a large hood over the front bay window on No. 12, a house very unlike its demure neighbours with a Gothic style that is more 'hair-raising horror novel' than 'medieval cathedral'. The first floor ends in pointed arches so steep they serve as a pair of exclamation marks. Half the façade is stone-clad, half bolstered by wooden beams and panels. The curved helmet roof on the window, whose leaded panes reach almost to the floor, is big, dark, shiny and inexplicable. It is as if the house has demanded your wallet and pulled out a blade. Under the window, the foundation stones include a plaque that addresses God and hopes 'the world may believe that thou hast sent me'. This dwelling is one of John Betjeman's destinations in the cult documentary *Metro-Land*. Betjeman tells with relish the tale of John Hugh Smyth-Pigott (see the entry on the Agapemonite Church on page 215), who owned the house in the nineteenth century. My money would be on the plaque having come from him. Later residents have included Charles Saatchi and Vanessa Feltz, who clearly fancied the cloak of eccentricity it confers upon any inhabitant. Langford Place is a cosseted little street hidden between Finchley Rd and Abbey Rd, where Beatles fans infuriate motorists by queueing up to re-enact the *Abbey Road* sleeve on the zebra crossing.

BOND STREET

TIME-LIFE SCREEN
1 Bruton Street, W1J 6TL

The buildings of Bond St are embellished with such variety that to walk its length feels like strolling through Ixelles. Atkinson's perfumers is splashed with gold leaf and heraldry, and its spire contains London's only carillon, while 179 New Bond St has a striking attic with a sunburst motif. At the other end, No. 71 has three excellent allegorical statues. *Art* and *Science* kowtow to the central figure of *Commerce*, which seems quite observant given the money changing hands in the flagship stores of designer labels. But if the art nouveau gets too sugary, turn to the Time-Life building on the corner of Bruton St, which houses a quartet of amorphous sculptures by Henry Moore. They sit in four openings on a screen wall, posed against the sky, and their typically inscrutable form is part humanoid, part Monster Munch. Moore was disgruntled when the architects declined to provide turntables for the stones to be rotated; he conceived of them 'project[ing] from the building like some of those half animals that look as if they are escaping through the walls in Romanesque reliefs'. Their positioning within a row of slots makes them look like the toy abacus of some gigantic child.

THE GODDESS SEKHMET
Sothebys, 34-35 New Bond Street, W1A 2AA

Sitting above the entrance to Sotheby's on New Bond St is one of the very oldest artefacts on the streets of London. Sekhmet, daughter of Ra, was a lion-headed goddess worshipped by the ancient Egyptians as the deity of war, fire, vengeance and menstruation (I'm saying nothing). This black basalt bust has been dated to 1320 BCE; legend has it that Sekhmet was sold for £40 in the 1880s, but her buyer never returned to collect. It certainly makes you wonder which works of European art might be serving as street furniture in 5000 CE. The first published work by the great travel writer Bruce Chatwin was a description of the piece; he joined Sotheby's as a porter and ended up a director. The auctioneers started out in 1804 as book dealers; a notable early acquisition was Napoleon's library from St Helena. Next door, No. 33 features some lovely friezes (not as old as they look) in which Odysseus sacrifices a ram.

THREE FIGURES
Bourdon Place, W1K 3AF

When I stumbled across this installation in an obscure converted mews in the middle of Mayfair, my first thought was that I had found the location for Antonioni's *Blow Up* (I was of course quite wrong: David Hemmings' studio was way out west). Here we have three bronzes. Their props are identifiable, but the people themselves are half-

sketched and look like Easter Island statues. A slender, gamine girl in a tie stands against the wall, tugging the hem of her dress in a mock curtsey. In the centre of the cobbled passage, a hunched photographer captures her image with intense concentration. At the top of the street, between two bollards, a woman laden with shopping bags appears to halt mid-stride and stand transfixed, as if asking herself 'Hang on, isn't that . . .?' A plaque informs us that the model is Twiggy, the photographer Terence Donovan, and the third party 'a passing shopper'. The triptych sounds like a recreation of some iconic photo from Swinging London, but it is entirely a product of the sculptor Neal French's imagination. Although Donovan had a studio at No. 30, he did not move here until 1978. The shopper is placed a few metres away from artist and model, making the whole street part of the work.

Their juxtaposition is interesting and, like a scene from Pinter, makes you consider the unequal power dynamics. Watching a woman watch a photographer watch a model makes you the last link in a chain of voyeurs.

QUEEN OF TIME
Selfridges, 400 Oxford Street, W1A 1AB

On Oxford St, you are more likely to hear the No. 73 bus splutter its way through the exhaust fumes of a tailback than time's winged chariot hurrying near. An upwards glance on the way into Selfridges, however, can still add a dash of panache to your shopping trip. Standing eleven feet tall on one of London's flagship department stores, the *Queen of Time* makes a glorious figurehead for this mercantile Mecca. Gilbert Bayes's sculpture is a polychromatic show of strength. Her tousled hair matches the bronze of her feathery wings, her flesh is burnished brass with a tint of honey, and her powder-blue dress hangs off her in long folds. The clock behind is blue-on-gold, its two faces tilting inwards. Stood on the prow of a ship, the queen gazes inscrutably at the horizon. In the background two angels with hammers tend to the clock's machinery, and two beautiful mermaids lie at her feet, each holding a crescent moon to signify her control over the tides. A Wisconsin man, Harry Gordon Selfridge coined the phrases 'the customer is always right' and 'only [xx] shopping days until Christmas'. Arriving in London in 1906, he devised Selfridges as a glamour destination that would turn shopping from a chore into a pleasure. After living it up with gambling sprees and dancing girls, Selfridge lost his fortune and died penniless in a rented flat in Putney. Should you like to see more of the *Queen of Time*, the model Leopoldine Avico also posed for the statue at Vintner's Place, on the north side of Southwark Bridge. Wearing nothing but a slightly manic grin, she is surrounded by adoring doves and goats.

WESTMINSTER

SHADOWS
Westminster Bridge, SW1A

Should you ever get a craving to see a hundred erect phalluses lined up before you, there's no need to trek out to distant car parks or woodlands. Seconds away from our seat of government, a free show is put on every day. Westminster Bridge is painted green to match the nearby House of Commons (just past Westminster, Lambeth Bridge is red to match the House of Lords). The iron bridge contains Gothic details by Charles Barry and is beloved by camera-wielding tourists for its close views of Parliament. All very dignified and appropriate for its privileged position; until 2007, that is. The bridge was repainted and architects were commissioned to replace

Barry's fascia pattern of sets of three intersecting circles in shamrock formation. When the new-look bridge was unveiled, it was discovered that around 1 p.m. on a sunny day, the sun hits the railing at a particular angle that elongates the upper circle and casts a row of identical phallic shadows onto the pavement, and there was much sniggering. Rumours soon emerged that the Mayor of London intended to close the bridge to all traffic and pedestrians in the early afternoon, obviously circulated by people who know nothing about the current Mayor of London.

TWENTIETH-CENTURY MARTYRS
Westminster Abbey, 20 Deans Yard, SW1P 3PA

Work began on Westminster Abbey as we know it in 1245; the present church is the third to have stood on this site. The building of Westminster Abbey spanned four centuries and its western towers were added by Hawksmoor in the eighteenth century. You may well do a double take after noticing that the Great West Door's Gothic niches contain some limestone statues of martyrs wearing glasses. The ten niches actually date from the fifteenth century, but were not filled until 1998. The modern martyrs span from China to Latin America, from the fame of Martin Luther King to the obscurity of a Papuan clergyman, from a Russian Tsarist princess to an African girl killed by her parents. In the central niches, Martin Luther King and Oscar Romero are joined by children; it is interesting to see the methods of modern PR applied to a medieval medium. Seeing this United Nations of the dead appear in covered alcoves is oddly reminiscent of sixties *Star Trek*. The choice of twentieth-century figures is a warning to learn lessons from that bloody century, and suggests that the story of Christianity should not end with the traditional saints if it wishes to stay relevant. Their diversity is reflective of London's current position as an international city, and serves to gently remind us that we are all essentially the same.

KINGS AND QUEENS
The Supreme Court, Parliament Square, Little George Street, SW1P 3BD

On Parliament Square it is Big Ben that draws most of the tourists' oohs and aahs, before they continue to the Thames or up Whitehall. Middlesex Guildhall takes something of a back seat but is worth a look for its unusual fusion of Gothic and art nouveau. The building was constructed in the years prior to World War I, just as one style was giving way to another. The carvings around its entrance are delectable; a slightly dreamy tapestry of solemn monarchs are presented with items on cushions, while ladies, courtiers and pageboys look on. Above the windows on the left is King John, about to affix his seal to the Magna Carta. Either side of him are two bishops, with a few hooded monks lurking behind. Barons in chainmail watch closely, their hands on their swords lest the sovereign has second thoughts. On the opposite side, a kneeling Duke of Suffolk offers the crown to Lady Jane Grey. If you're wondering how this turned out, the National Gallery has a very good Delaroche painting about it. The centre shows Henry III granting a charter to Westminster Abbey, whose belfry stood on this site. Above, Britannia is flanked by allegorical female figures, and the balcony on the side of the building finds oddly voluptuous angels acting as corbels. It is intriguing that the three monarchs chosen were all brought low by circumstance; the implication is that not even a divinely appointed king is above the law. The sculptor was H. C. Fehr, whose work can also be seen on Russell Square's voluminous Hotel Russell, where he provided statues of four English queens.

BOMB SHELTER SIGNS
7 Lord North Street, SW1P 3LA

Tucked in between Westminster, Millbank, Victoria St and Horseferry Rd is a network of handsome streets composed of tall Georgian terraces. These make up a prime residential slice of the so-called 'Westminster Bubble'. On Lord North St, therefore, it is a surprise to find remnants of a time when we were slightly more in it together. Stencilled onto the bricks in black paint are large arrows bearing the legend 'Public shelters in vaults under pavements in this street'. One half expects to follow the arrows and find Secret Cinema charging £30 for a teacup of gin and a screening of *London Can Take It*, but the signs are authentic. At No. 4 lived Lord Anderson, wartime Home Secretary who gave his name to the Anderson shelter; some 3.6 million of these six-person shelters were distributed across the country. Harold Wilson also lived here while prime minister, his wife having refused 10 Downing St and insisted on 'a proper home'. The street ends at Smith Square, with the Italianate church of St John at its centre. The church features lofty towers on each of its four corners, earning it the contemporary nickname 'Queen Anne's footstool'. Proving the efficacy of bomb shelters, St John's was denuded of its roof in the Blitz and left in ruins until 1965, when it was restored and converted into a concert hall.

SOUTHWARK

DOG AND POT
Southwark Station, 68–70 Blackfriars Road, SE1 8JZ

Charles Dickens was all his life an intemperate walker. His essay *Night Walks* relates how he would sometimes spend the whole night tramping the streets of London as a result of his insomnia. The people he encountered, the details he noticed and the unending diversity of the city fired the novelist's imagination from an early age. At twelve years old, Dickens saw his father imprisoned and the boy's education was cut short for a stint at a blacking (boot polish) factory. He later recalled his walk to work along Blackfriars Rd, passing 'the likeness of a golden dog licking a golden pot over a shop door'; the dog and pot was a symbol common to ironmongers, as iron bars used in fireplaces were called 'dogs'. Outside Southwark Tube station, before a small lawn you will find a Victorian lamp post, atop which perches a golden-brown dog feasting on the contents of an upturned cooking pot. This replica of the sign Dickens walked past was installed in 2013 to commemorate his 200th birthday, and unveiled by his descendant Mark Dickens. The ironmongers' workshop is long gone, but the original dog and pot sign resides at the Cuming Museum on Walworth Rd.

LONDON BRIDGE

FERRYMAN'S SEAT
Riverside House, Southwark Bridge Road, SE1 9HA

London has over twenty bridges today but for the vast majority of its history London Bridge stood alone. Beyond the City boundaries, the South Bank was a licentious strip that served Londoners with brothels, booze, bear-baiting and (worst of all) theatre. Congested with homes and shop units, London Bridge had a roadway of just four metres. Wherrymen, who could row people back and forth, were much in demand. On the corner of Bankside and Bear Gardens, now built into the side of a chain restaurant, is the Ferryman's Seat, an inscrutable apparition from London's past. The watermen would sit here and wait for their vessels to fill up with passengers, then take them back to the City for a small fee. In an attempt to impose order on the chaotic river traffic, Henry VIII gave the watermen exclusive licence to carry passengers across. A company was formed, and the watermen had to serve a seven-year apprenticeship studying the tides and currents of the Thames. Their work became scarce in the winters of the late seventeenth century, when London Bridge restricted the flow of the Thames so much that it would commonly freeze, allowing people simply to walk over it. Under a plaque that speaks vaguely of 'ancient origins', the tiny stone seat has chipped, scratched and eroded to the point that there is not much left to see. Attached to a sleek new building, it looks like some startled plant pulled out by its roots, and hastily shoved into new soil. Anyone occupying it today is more likely to be posing for a holiday photo than saying, 'You'll never guess who I had in the back of my skiff yesterday, guv.'

V2 ROCKET
64 Tooley Street, SE1 2TF

A few metres east of London Bridge at its southern end is a sliver of a five-storey building. Hanging from its narrow side is a white rocket, emblazoned with 'V2'. In the final months of World War II, Wernher von Braun's demonic creations rained terror onto London and a V2 explosion in nearby Borough High St killed thirty-five people, making the installation of this rocket a curious decision at best. It was put here to advertise a now-defunct museum on the site, the snappily titled 'Winston Churchill's Britain at War Experience'. Budding Thunderbirds will tell you that the rocket is actually a model of a NASA Atlas, presumably acquired from a planetarium. Having outstayed the museum, it would be nice to think that this uncanny London anomaly might survive the current redevelopment of London Bridge station and the surrounding area, but the odds are stacked against it. While the rocket clings on to its residency, the best views are from platform 1 of the station.

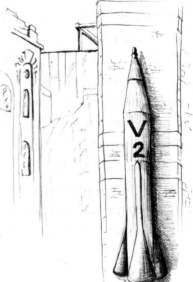

ART-DECO WOMAN
Adelaide House, London Bridge, EC4R 9HA

Consisting of a modest eleven floors, this building at the northern end of London Bridge seems eminently grounded when one glances across the Thames to the Shard. It is surprising to learn that when the current Adelaide House (the second on this site) opened in 1926, it was the tallest block in the City. Bringing an American influence to London, it featured such innovations as air conditioning and a putting green on the roof. The stone is studded with stars. A strangely sombre woman stands guard above the art-deco pillars and gates of the entrance, holding a globe with the symbols of the zodiac. Her head is covered and symmetrical folds in her robes frame the sculpture. The work feels quite formal; it is no surprise to learn that William Reid Dick, the artist responsible, specialized in war memorials. She is a wistful addition to a remnant of the Roaring Twenties that can easily be missed by workers hurrying towards the station. Indeed, the building squeezes into the narrow space in front of St Magnus Martyr like a bowler-hatted businessman nipping onto the 18:06 to Orpington just before the doors shut. This church, now concealed behind Adelaide House, is also worth a look. One of Wren's most beautiful interiors, it today cleaves to the Anglo-Catholic tradition and contains all kinds of decidedly un-Protestant icons.

BERMONDSEY

LEATHERMARKET ROUNDELS
11-13 Weston Street, SE1 3ER

Bermondsey came to prominence as the place that supplied Britain with its leather. Butchers would bring their hides to a leather exchange for inspection and trade, any wool or hair on the animal skin being kept aside for millinery. A gory business, and one grimaces to imagine the unsanitary conditions that prevailed. As the industry grew, in 1833 a large market opened on Weston Street, where tanners could buy hides and sell their leather. It is a low-key complex, but the building on the corner serves as its showpiece. Two morose musclemen (one bearded, one not) hold up a porch, emblazoned with 'London Leather, Hide & Wool Exchange'. The keystone in the arch is another bearded face surrounded by garlands. Above the ground floor windows are five roundels, with carvings that depict the process of leather-making. We see workers scraping hair and flesh from the hides, the hides soaking in oak bark, the tanned leather rolled by hand, and finally gentlemen purchasing the finished product. The craftsmanship and detail of these carvings shows the Industrial Revolution in its boom years. Manufacturing is given the attention that would previously have been given to Bible stories, and there is an emphasis on showing where the product came from. British leather is more of an artisan business now, and most of our leather comes from China and Italy.

Metropolitan Line

Within a few minutes of your train leaving Baker Street or Marylebone, London ends and the Shires begin. The Paris Metro takes its name after the Metropolitan Railway, which opened in 1863, connecting Paddington to the City. Soon it was spilling out into Middlesex, and wherever it went, suburbia followed. Eulogized by John Betjeman and Julian Barnes, 'Metroland' is as much a state of mind as it is a place. The railwaymen were selling a dream: a lifestyle that promised all the benefits of country living with the capital just a fast train journey away. Even the handles of train-carriage doors once exhorted passengers to 'Live in Metro-land'. Like New York or Dubai, London is now a world city, arguably the capital of Europe, and has more in common with the globalized world than with its host country. If you are used to skyscrapers and the inner city, taking the Metropolitan line to one of the old market towns of Buckinghamshire can be as unfamiliar and exotic as flying to Ulaanbaatar.

FINCHLEY ROAD

SIGMUND FREUD'S COUCH
Freud House Museum, 20 Maresfield Gardens, NW3 5SX

With the Holocaust, Europe was deprived of a vital and significant component of its culture, one which bequeathed to us Kafka, Mahler and Einstein among others. Britain is the custodian of a few fragments of this lost world. The Warburg Institute is one, another is the Freud family home, packed up and transported from Berggasse 19, Vienna, to 20 Maresfield Gardens, NW3. The Freud family had initially hoped to remain in Vienna, but the arrest of daughter Anna after the *Anschluss* made clear the danger of doing so. The house is now a museum, its star attraction Freud's consulting room preserved exactly as it was. You could be forgiven for thinking that the father of psychoanalysis has just stepped outside, and the experience is as eerie as entering a pharaoh's tomb. Draped in cushions and an oriental rug, the famous couch is where patients would lie to be analysed. With Freud out of sight behind the head of the couch, they would discuss their dreams and childhood memories, and practise the free-association technique. Psychoanalysis has its naysayers but there can be no doubt that Freud's ideas have shaped our thoughts for a hundred years. The study is now a secular shrine and the couch its most valuable relic. Very few pieces of soft furnishing can be said to have changed history, but this is one of them.

WEMBLEY PARK

WATKIN'S FOLLY
Wembley Stadium, HA9 0WS

When Wembley Stadium lost its twin turrets and was rebuilt in the early years of this century, builders uncovered the foundations of what, had things turned out differently, might have been London's most famous landmark. You will not be able to see the remains of Watkin's Tower, as they are currently covered over by the hallowed turf of the football pitch. But next time you watch England beat Tajikistan 1–0 in front of a half-empty crowd of corporate sponsors, use your imagination to conjure up a spectacular tower, far taller than the Shard, that straddles the north-west London skyline. Sir Edward Watkin was a railway entrepreneur of unbridled ambition who started building a Channel tunnel to France in 1881. One year in, the government became nervous about the implications for defence of the realm and made him stop. To entice more Londoners into the countryside and onto his trains, he decided to build a huge amusement park, Wembley Park. Its centrepiece was to be a huge tower, some fifty metres taller than the Eiffel Tower, and accommodating a hotel, sanatorium, theatres, gardens and Turkish bath. When Gustave Eiffel himself declined the job, Watkin held a design competition. All kinds of preposterous plans were submitted, including replicas of the Great Giza Pyramid and the Tower of Pisa; the winning entry was suspiciously similar to La Tour Eiffel. The first section of the tower was built by 1895, with the surrounding park proving a popular visitor attraction, but that was as good as it got. Ill health compelled Watkin to retire and without the propeller of his energy, the project remained unfinished. The killer blow came when its foundations began to subside into the marshy ground of Wembley. The aborted tower's first level was left to rust for thirteen years before being put out of its misery.

HARROW-ON-THE-HILL

HARROW SCHOOL
5 High Street, HA1 3HP

From Harrow-on-the-Hill station there are two exits. One leads to Novosibirsk, the other to Assisi. Harrow's modern town centre is a charmless swamp of office blocks, flyovers, multi-storey car parks and shopping malls, but head instead for the summit and you find the polar opposite: a very scenic old hilltop town built around the famous school. The spire of St Mary's is planted on the pinnacle; sections of the church tower date to William the Conqueror's reign. The curving High St follows the ridge of the hill. Leave St Mary's via the churchyard and you will descend into an unexpectedly breathtaking spectacle. As you stand on a stone balcony, with flights of wide stairs leading to street level on either side, the grandest buildings of Harrow School surround you. The Old School of 1615 has a cupola clock between the stepped gables of each wing. George Gilbert Scott added a flint-clad chapel and the polychromatic brick patterns of the library. This boys' boarding school is one of Britain's most prestigious and has provided seven prime ministers, including Churchill. The old tuck shop on the High St still sells upmarket marmalades and chocolates, and you may well see pupils in straw hats or morning coats. Any foreign visitors mesmerized by tales of the Bullingdon Club will lap up this stuff, and they are catered for by the tearooms and outfitters further along the street's twists and turns. The promenade of rustic cottages ends in a small village green, with an old gantry sign that contains a portrait of Henry VIII.

RAYNERS LANE

ZOROASTRIAN CENTRE
440 Alexandra Avenue, HA2 9TL

The golden age of cinema firmly behind us, the uses to which our prettiest remaining art-deco cinemas are currently put can be distressing. They are more likely than not to house a Hard Rock Café or a Wetherspoon pub. It is not all bad news, however. In May 2015 Regent Street cinema, which screened the reels of the Lumière brothers in 1896, reopened its doors after a thirty-five-year hiatus. Out on Alexandra Avenue, it is heartening to note that one gorgeous cinema is now a place of worship for the Zoroastrians. This eminent faith was the religion of the great Persian empires that coexisted alongside ancient Rome, long before the Islamic conquest of Iran. Since then, adherents have been a minority wherever they are found. For centuries the faith has been kept alive by Parsis, who migrated to India (famous Parsis include Freddie Mercury and the conductor Zubin Mehta). This is their only European base. The building is a handsome example of the 'streamline moderne' style, with a façade in three bow-shaped parts. The outer sections feature long columns of convex windows, while the windows on the central part curve inwards. Between its two columns of glass is a curved piece of concrete that unfolds from the roof down to the entrance canopy and is known as the 'elephant's trunk' for its distinctive shape. The building opened as the Grosvenor Cinema in 1936, changing hands a few times before becoming a nightclub. It was left vacant for a few years until 2000, when the Zoroastrians moved in. The interior features uplighting and a proscenium arch marked with the Zoroastrian faravahar, a spirit guide within a winged disc, plus the motto 'Good thoughts, good deeds, good words'.

UXBRIDGE

STAINED GLASS
Uxbridge Station, High Street, UB8 1JZ

Stations at the end of the line have an atmosphere quite distinct from the others, one of quiet melancholy. This is the limit of the city's dominion; past here, you're on your own. At Uxbridge, terminus for Metropolitan and Piccadilly lines, London bids the passenger farewell in style, with a station by Charles Holden, the architect who created so much with so little for the north-east stations of the Piccadilly line. At its entrance are a pair of modernist sculptures: winged wheels to ennoble a passenger's journey from Hillingdon to Holborn with a sense of magic. Even more arresting are the three panels of stained glass above the concourse, with heraldic arms and brilliant colours that sprinkle a scintilla of the Sainte Chapelle over suburbia. At the centre is the coat of arms of Uxbridge district council, which merged with other councils in 1965. To the sides, a crown over three blades represents Middlesex, with a swan for Buckinghamshire. The pattern connecting the crests contains leaves, feathers and interlocking diamond patterns that resemble tartan. The artist was Ervin Bossányi, a Hungarian Jew who fled Hamburg for England in 1934. The glasswork is the kind more commonly seen in medieval churches, to the point where it appears quite unreal placed within Holden's linear concrete modernism. Indeed, more of Bossányi's designs can be seen in the cathedrals of York, Ely, Canterbury and Washington D.C.

London Overground

The Overground is to the Circle line as Vienna's Gürtel is to its Ringstrasse. It may not contain as much in the way of tourist sights, but it covers the areas further out, where London's workforce can actually afford to live. The loop around London's edges is a cobbling together of older services with bits of new track. The stretch running from Dalston through to Kilburn and Willesden was formerly the Silverlink or North London line, and the Highbury to Crystal Palace/Croydon section is a souped-up and extended East London line. Trains run a little less frequently than on the Underground but the carriages are spacious and air-conditioned. The past ten years have seen a great migration to the extremities of south-east and north-east London, as rents elsewhere soar far beyond people's reach, and a frequent train service in areas not traditionally blessed with one became an urgent necessity. The Overground locations are now catching up with the rest, and Crossrail will draw outlying districts like Woolwich, Forest Gate and even Reading into the equation.

CANONBURY

WADDINGTON STUDIOS
127 Church Walk, N16 8QW

Albion Rd is a narrow, congested road that was not designed for the volume of traffic it now receives. I walked to work along its miserly slender pavements for a ridiculously long time before realizing that there is another, much quieter street running parallel, beginning at the Unitarian church on Newington Green and returning the pedestrian to the outside world at the Trinitarian church. Church Walk is an enclosed, secret little sanctuary; like the best mews, but adding incredible variety in a very short space. In just a few minutes it draws you down the rabbit hole, past a whole gamut of styles and out again. There are allotments, car mechanics, a school and stencil paintings of local heroes and villains (Mary Wollstonecraft, Malcolm McLaren) while housing ranges from council blocks and Victorian terracing to avant-garde glass boxes and wood cabins. To discover it is akin to walking into the wings at a theatre and seeing stage sets from various productions propped idly against the walls. The most striking of the new buildings is halfway down Church Walk. Waddington Studios, a photography studio with flats beneath, has replaced a factory run by the card manufacturers of the same name. The front is covered with large sheets of metal, rusted orange and perforated with small holes in patterns that echo playing cards. Jutting out over the top edge, more like an iceberg than a ship's prow, is a trapezoid box posed at a sharp angle, a loose chain dangling from its base. One edge contains a large window, but approach it from the other side and you might think a shipping container has slipped out of a crane's grasp; the flattened remains of some poor stevedore could be underneath. The street being invisible from without, it is probably easier to get planning permission for more outlandish designs.

DALSTON KINGSLAND

RUINED CHAPEL
Abney Park Cemetery, Stoke Newington High Street, N16 0LH

Stoke Newington, in its days as a country retreat, was home of the Dissenters. Now tamed by gentrification, it proudly upheld this dissenter tradition in subsequent eras. Key feminist Mary Wollstonecraft was a regular at Newington Green's Unitarian church, which was visited by David Hume, Adam Smith, and some of America's Founding Fathers. Terrorist cell the Angry Brigade operated from a base at 359 Amhurst Rd in the 1970s. Abney Park Cemetery, opened in 1840, was a resting place for non-conformists. Like Highgate and Nunhead cemeteries, the foliage and weeds grow free, creating an overgrown look. The cemetery's most famous resident is William Booth, founder of the Salvation Army, and there is a statue of Isaac Watts, who lived on the grounds and whose 700-odd hymns include 'Joy to the World'. Concealed at the heart of Abney Park is the ruined structure of a small Gothic revival church. Its steeple is large and plain, its walls unassuming brick, and not much else is left. Large rose windows and pointed arch windows are bereft of any glass. The fittings are long gone and the skeleton of the church has returned to the wild. An old rumour about Satanist rites in the church resurfaces now and again: people report pentagrams and upside-down crosses daubed on its inner walls, but they could come from one of the many music videos shot here. The chapel made the national press in 2014 when a community chairman complained of 'drug-fuelled orgies' and groups 'copulating on tombstones'. Funnily enough, he turned out to be a self-publishing novelist who writes erotic thrillers. Eventually the council made the eminently sensible decision that this unsafe structure should be closed off to the public. If any men in the park stop walking as you pass and try to make eye contact, my advice is to look straight ahead and keep walking.

HACKNEY CENTRAL

AGAPEMONITE ANIMALS
Georgian Orthodox Church, Rookwood Road, N16 6SS

Follow the 'murder mile' of Lower and Upper Clapton Rd away from Hackney, and by Clapton Common you will spot a fairly striking church on Rookwood Rd. Built in dark stone with Portland stone trim and a needle spire, what marks it out as unusual is the bestiary of large sculptures dotted around its exterior. Perched on turrets around the base of the spire, looking out towards the four compass points, are bronzes of the four evangelists: an ox, an eagle, a lion and a man, each with a cumbersome pair of outstretched wings. Further down are larger-still representations of the quartet, emerging from the stone and looking quite modernist. Each tramples upon a contorted and defeated-looking human. If you detect a smidgen of unconventionality here, you're not wrong. Today a Georgian Orthodox church, this was built in the 1890s for the Agapemonites, a cult whose leaders advocated a chaste 'spiritual marriage', segregating their flock but taking multiple wives themselves at their 'abode of love' in Somerset. It was at Clapton that their second leader, John Hugh Smyth-Pigott, announced himself as the Messiah, provoking a riot when he then failed to walk across the common's ponds. Back towards Hackney is another beautiful and unusual church, the Round Chapel, near the start of Lower Clapton Rd.

LONDON BRIDGE
Victoria Park, Grove Road, E3 5TB

London is a Roman city. When Emperor Claudius' troops swept aside the native tribes of Britain, on the way to Colchester they used a temporary pontoon bridge to cross the Thames, and London grew up around this site. Timber bridges came and went until 1209, when the first London Bridge in stone, thirty-three years in the making, was completed. It looked very different from the London Bridge we know now; there were buildings along both sides, some seven storeys high. Its Victorian replacement started to sink and was sold for just over a million pounds (the current bridge dates from 1973). The granite masonry was transported to Arizona and rebuilt. Londoners like to say that the ill-informed buyer had mistaken London Bridge for the more flamboyant Tower Bridge, which speaks volumes about our anxiety at being overtaken by the 'new money' of the United States. You can still see a component of the medieval London Bridge four miles north-east, in Victoria Park, the great green space of the East End that has long been a meeting place for activists and pleasure-seekers alike. When London Bridge's buildings were demolished, the Georgians installed fourteen covered stone alcoves between balustrades, in the shape of semi-dome apses. When the bridge was taken down two of these ended up in Hackney, to the eternal gratitude of any passers-by caught out by a sudden storm.

SHOREDITCH HIGH STREET

ACTORS' MEMORIAL
St Leonard's C of E Church, Shoreditch High Street, E1 6JN

That Nathan Barley, like his spiritual fathers New Labour, does not 'do God' can be surmised from a glance at the parlous condition of St Leonard's, found where Old Street, Kingsland Road and Hackney Road converge. Its neighbour, Hawksmoor's Christchurch, was lovingly restored with much time and money and St Leonard's looks like it could also do with some TLC. There has been a church here since Saxon times and the current one was built in 1736. As in the rhyme 'Oranges and Lemons', the bells of Shoreditch parley with their London neighbours. The tall steeple, with a needlepoint emerging from a round colonnade, echoes St Mary-le-Bow and the four Tuscan columns in its portico are akin to St Paul's in Covent Garden. At the moment, half the portico is cordoned off because of the risk of falling masonry. The rear window is covered by a wire grille and the whole building could be some big Venetian palazzo, another chunk dropping off as each speedboat zooms past. Like Covent Garden, this is something of an actors' church. Inside, an Edwardian marble plaque remembers some of the thespians buried here; on nearby Curtain Rd, James Burbage founded 'The Theatre', England's second permanent theatre. Shakespeare employed Burbage's son, Richard, as the leading man for many of his great tragedies, and his other son Cuthbert founded the original Globe Theatre on the South Bank. Although the church looks as crumbly as shortbread, its gardens are still well tended and well used.

I AM YOUR FATHER
35–45 Great Eastern Street, EC2A 3ER

The secret of capitalism's endurance is its ability to take any form of challenge from counter-culture and repackage it as a product for sale. A good example is the twenty-first-century phenomenon of the celebrity graffiti artist. Taking to the streets instead of the galleries, they worked in anonymity and outside of the official channels, but their popularity has led to official commissions, book deals and films. Property owners excavate and auction the hallowed piece of wall, the system absorbs the dissenting voice and finds a way to make money from it. Such success is 'a mark of failure for a graffiti artist', says Banksy, apparently worth over £12 million. You may have noticed one of the 150 or so 'Space Invaders' dotted around London. These small and simple mosaics consist of a few large square tiles, resembling the large pixels of a primitive computer game, representing a Pac-man as often as a Space Invader. These are the work of one 'Invader', a Parisian who travels the world leaving his work on city walls. If they seem slightly banal, rest assured that there are plenty of critics ready to assert that this postmodern tiling re-contextualizes the built environment. At the rear of a multi-storey car park on Shoreditch's Curtain Rd, one diverting example of his work sees a pixelated Luke Skywalker and Darth Vader re-enact their famous light sabre duel from *The Empire Strikes Back*. Perhaps this piece finds Invader working through some issues after being told that Charles Saatchi is his father.

GOAT
Brushfield Street, E1 6AA

A dozen years ago, Spitalfields market was closer in spirit to Camden than it was to the luxury retail expected by the nearby City. Unable to expand southwards because of the river, the City has been gradually cannibalizing chunks of the East End since, and the Spitalfields area feels increasingly sanitized. The area to the rear of the market has been tarted up as Bishop's Square: glass-fronted buildings, stone benches around a lily-pad pond, and yet more privately owned public space. With local government no longer able to afford the maintenance of its property, this trend is sure to go on gathering speed. A section of glass pavement shows the remains of a fourteenth-century charnel house beneath street level, so the area does at least have a good track record for dead things. As a small concession to humanity, one end of the complex features a little white goat with horns and wispy beard, standing on a tall stack of packing boxes. The Scottish sculptor, Kenny Hunter, chose a goat for the animal's independent streak. It represents the minorities – Huguenot, Jew, Bangladeshi, George Galloway – who have successively made this area their home, while the precarious tower of crates, looking ready to collapse, aptly represents the turbulence of the economy. Developers do love paying lip service to an area's history while disinfecting the place to within an inch of its life. At the end of Brushfield St, Hawksmoor's Christchurch steeple is forever staring down the skyscrapers around it, like David slaying Goliath; the goat turns the tables on Christchurch.

WHITECHAPEL

SPIEGELHALTER'S
81 Mile End Road, E1 4UJ

The story of Spiegelhalter's is as uplifting as any you will find in London. Scant surprise, then, that property developers are trying to get rid of it. Its story is intertwined with that of the other family business that shared this block; the Spiegelhalters were jewellers and clockmakers, the Wickhams were drapers. As the Wickham empire expanded they bought up more units in the block, and in the 1920s decided to turn the whole thing into a 'Harrods of the East', drawing up plans for an opulent department store. Everyone on the block sold up, except the Spiegelhalters at No. 81 Mile End Rd. Assuming that they would see sense in time, the Wickhams built the rest of their building, leaving a gap around the Spiegelhalter shop that could be filled in later. This never happened, as Spiegelhalter's outlived the department store by some twenty years. Today we still see a long, imperious façade in dark stone, with Ionic columns and an odd, rectangular Hawksmoor-like tower, interrupted just past its halfway point by a shabby little shopfront, painted white and bereft of any adornment. It is like seeing a Hollywood actress's smile after an incisor tooth has been knocked out. The neo classical posturing of Wickham's is made to look ridiculous, especially as that elaborate tower is forced to sit slightly off-centre. It is the architectural equivalent of Accrington Stanley beating Chelsea in a cup tie, and it cannot fail to raise a smile. In today's age of compulsory purchase orders, this could never happen again. Those who knew Spiegelhalter's remember a smart little shop, with curved glass and a mosaic floor; in expectation of permission to redevelop, however, new developers have demolished it all, leaving only the front wall. Their ultimate aim is to remove every trace of the shop and build a glass atrium behind the Wickham's façade. A spectacular exercise in point-missing is summed up neatly by their observation that 'the attractiveness and uniformity of 69–89 Mile End Road is marred only by 81 Mile End Road which is inferior in appearance, detailing and architecture'. It will be a sad day for London if they get their way.

EAGLES
Malplaquet House, 137 Mile End Road, E1 4AQ

Mile End Rd, with its large Asian community, retail parks and many chicken shops, has changed a lot since 1742 when Malplaquet House was built. Presumably built for a Georgian merchant, and subsequently lived in by widows, surgeons and brewers, it is stately, unpretentious and very likeable. For years this was a shop specializing in typewriter repairs; instead of a front garden there were shop units, and the fine house was largely obscured by the shabby façade of this extension. Today, a wall and a dense jungle garden replete with palm trees create a barrier between the house and the traffic-heavy road. The two tall pillars either side of the gate are capped by a majestic pair of Napoleonic-looking eagles, wings half-stretched and heads held high, as if the house behind is the source of their pride. Their beaks lend a hint of menace to a house that visitors always seem to compare to Miss Havisham's home in *Great Expectations*. In a derelict state by the 1990s and housing only pigeons, Malplaquet House was carefully restored to Georgian grace by a landscaper and the director of the Sir John Soane Museum, who filled it with remarkable antique items. The change is astonishing – caterpillar to butterfly.

WAPPING

TIGER AND BOY
Tobacco Dock, Tobacco Quay, Wapping Lane, E1W 2SF

A literary hit in 2011, Carol Birch's novel *Jamrach's Menagerie* rekindled interest in the story of Charles Jamrach, an enterprising German with a famous shop in the East End. Located close to London's bustling docks, Jamrach imported exotic animals for sale to zoos, circuses and wealthy private collectors, and was enough of a celebrity to make an appearance in Bram Stoker's

Dracula. At the entrance to Tobacco Dock, a former warehouse on Wapping Lane, a cute statue depicts a dramatic incident from the entrepreneur's life. In 1857 a Bengal tiger escaped from the emporium. When a small boy tried to pet it, the tiger carried him off in its jaws and Jamrach was only able to save the boy by forcing his arm down the tiger's throat. The bronze statue, perhaps owing something to Walt Disney's rendering of Shere Khan and Mowgli, commemorates this encounter, with the tiger looming over a mesmerized boy and ready to swipe. The boy's parents prosecuted Jamrach, who had to pay £300 for his trouble. In 1980 a near-derelict Tobacco Dock was used by Orchestral Manoeuvres in the Dark for their 'Messages' video; in the 1990s it was converted into a shopping mall and spectacularly failed in its mission to become the 'Covent Garden of the East'. The site still proves useful on occasion; during the 2012 Olympics it became a barracks for 2,500 soldiers.

HANGMAN'S NOOSE
Prospect of Whitby, 57 Wapping Wall, E1W 3SH

Between the death of Charles II and the Glorious Revolution, England endured an uneasy three years with Charles's Catholic brother James II on the throne. His reign was marked by rebellions and clashes with Anglicans, and in these his chief enforcer was Judge Jeffreys, known as 'the hanging judge'. Following an abortive revolt in 1685,

Jeffreys presided over the trials with such severity that they were called the 'Bloody Assizes'. Hundreds were hanged, and hundreds more transported to Barbados (which doesn't seem the most arduous sentence today). Jeffreys' local was the Prospect of Whitby on Wapping High St, which looks onto the stretch of riverbank known as Execution Dock. Here pirates were hanged with a short rope to ensure a slow death by strangulation. The judge is reputed to have enjoyed watching the hangings while eating lunch here. To remind people of the pub's lurid place in history, just below the rear balcony stands a gallows with noose, which for the moment is not being put to use. The pub's stone floors date from its establishment in 1520, although much of the building was reconstructed after a nineteenth-century fire. It is an atmospheric place with timber beams and panelling, and the terrace offers fine views of the river. As for Jeffreys, although James II fled to France, his favourite magistrate left it too late. He was found disguised as a sailor in the Town of Ramsgate (another extant riverside pub, just the other side of Wapping station) and taken to the Tower of London, where he died of kidney failure.

ROTHERHITHE

EDWARD III'S MANOR HOUSE
Bermondsey Wall East, SE16 4NB

In his fifty-year reign, King Edward III sailed England through some choppy waters, including the Black Death and battles against the Scottish/French alliance that would calcify into the Hundred Years War. To recuperate, the King had a manor house in Rotherhithe, then a country retreat on marshland downriver from the City. There was no hunting to be had here, but historians think he may have come to practise falconry. The house was later sold off and incorporated into warehouses, but the Docklands redevelopment of the 1980s uncovered some of its remains. These can be seen today, on a grassy mound between the Thames path and a row of nondescript terracing. The base of the front wall and its corners protrude from the grass like wisdom teeth. On a small island in the marshes, the house would have faced directly onto the Thames with a moat around the other three sides. Its remains strike an incongruous note. Children use them as a climbing frame while their parents drink in the Angel pub opposite. The Angel has been here since the fifteenth century; the current building is Regency and feels very old-fashioned, as opposed to the usual heritage parody. It is managed by Sam Smith's, who can generally be relied upon to neither ruin pubs nor turn them into expensive restaurants masquerading as pubs.

Its small riverside balcony is where Turner sat to paint *The Fighting Temeraire* and it still offers a marvellous, if melancholy, view of the Thames. Hugging the towers of Tower Bridge are the Post Office Tower and the dome of St Paul's. Bracketing this trio and looming over them like birds of prey are the new breed: on one side the Shard, on the other the Walkie-Talkie, the Cheese Grater and the Gherkin. From here you can see London cannibalize itself. Nearer Rotherhithe station, the Mayflower is another historic pub, named after the pilgrim ship that fatefully landed on Plymouth Rock.

DR SALTER'S DAYDREAM
Bermondsey Wall East, SE16 4NB

Before the remains of Edward III's house (see above), the riverside seating for overspill from the Angel features a discreet and unexpectedly moving quartet of bronze statues. You first notice an old man with trilby, glasses and cane, seated facing the Thames, with no explanatory plaque or label. Then you see a woman in period dress, standing off to his left. Both are watching a small girl lean against the wall, on which a cat sits. This is the Salter family. Dr Alfred Salter was an award-winning physician at Guy's Hospital and the Lister Institute. He and his wife Ada devoted their lives to improving conditions in the poverty-stricken slums of Bermondsey. They held some controversial views: Salter published a pamphlet opposing

World War I and resigned from the local Labour party over attempts to block Mosley's blackshirt marches. He represented the area in Parliament for over twenty years, and Ada was Bermondsey's first female mayor; they were respected for lowering the infant mortality rate by more than half, and their health centres are now considered 'an NHS before the NHS'. Their daughter Joyce died of scarlet fever at the age of eight. The statues depict Salter in his twilight years, remembering his family – or perhaps being called to rejoin them. When the figure of Dr Salter was cruelly stolen for scrap metal in 2011, locals immediately raised £60,000 to have him replaced and added the statue of Ada.

NEW CROSS GATE

FOUR ADMIRALS
Deptford Town Hall Building, SE14 6AF

A short hop from Greenwich, this exuberant Edwardian building makes quite a noise about Deptford's seafaring credentials. The maritime theme is everywhere, from a golden galleon acting as weathervane to the decorative anchors and navigational tools. Holding aloft the bow windows above a recessed doorway are two muscular mermen who would not look out of place on the imperial palaces of Habsburg Vienna. Taking pride of place on the façade are statues of four admirals in detailed period costume: Sir Francis Drake, Cromwell's commander Robert Blake, Horatio Nelson and a nameless contemporary sailor. Drake is in a neck ruffle and tights, with a globe at his feet; Nelson can be identified by his bicorne and his sleeve tucked inside his coat. The Town Hall now belonging to the right-on Goldsmiths College, some academics have expressed anxiety that this building is an apology for empire and the slave trade; an unsubstantiated rumour has it that the weathervane represents a slave ship. Anyone wishing to further contemplate this thorny legacy may continue to nearby Telegraph Hill Park, where schoolchildren have constructed a memorial plinth to Olaudah Equiano. The author of *The Interesting Narrative* passed through Deptford while enslaved to a naval lieutenant.

PECKHAM RYE

EDWARD VIII POSTBOX
Nunhead Green, SE15 3QF

When museums gather together busts or statues of Roman leaders, the 'bad emperors' tend to be in short supply; unpopular monarchs would have their statues destroyed or recut in the image of a successor. The turbulent three-year reign of Caligula has left us with less than fifty images, of which only the handful locked away after his death were not mutilated. To compare King Edward VIII to Caligula is probably unfair on Caligula, but the conventional view is that both reigns were regrettable. There was no official programme to smash up the remnants of the king's tenure after his shock abdication, although people must have been sorely tempted when he and Mrs Simpson paid a visit to Hitler. Ten months after his coronation, the abdication came so soon that there are similarly few surviving artefacts. British postboxes are usually marked with the cypher of the monarch at the time and a small number of Edward VIII postboxes linger on our streets. This postbox is on the corner of Nunhead Lane and Brock St. Others can be found on the Highway in Wapping, Wanstead Park Rd in Redbridge, the Grove in Stratford, Elliot Rd in Hendon and Waggon Rd in Barnet. Letter boxes came into use in 1852 at the suggestion of the novelist Anthony Trollope, who was working as a Post Office surveyor at the time.

FOREST HILL

FAÇADE WITH MOSAIC
Horniman Museum & Gardens, 100 London Road, SE23 3PQ

A perennial favourite for school trips, this museum may garner fewer accolades than its competitors because of its Forest Hill location, but the treasures within are deserving of a visit. The Horniman opened in 1901 to showcase the collections of the world's biggest tea merchant; today's exhibits focus on natural history, music and African artefacts. Its most famous resident is an outsize walrus, stuffed in the nineteenth century by a taxidermist who had never seen a living one and filled out the wrinkles. The building's exterior brings a hothouse exoticism to SE23. Palm trees stand before a sandcastle façade that is all smooth curves and mosaics. The façade is in two parts. One has a triangular church-like gable and, beneath, a sloping porch roof between two pavilions. The other is crowned by a pleasing curve that follows its barrel-vaulted ceiling, and attached to this is a tall, four-sided clock tower with rounded edges. A circular disc runs around its summit, with four spherical turrets on top; it looks as if Victor Horta had gone on holiday to Sicily, and is made stranger by its resolutely suburban location. The stone is embossed with the name of the museum, and beneath is an excellent mosaic, 9 metres by 3, in the Arts and Crafts style. The pastel-coloured tiles have a Roman look. Beautiful boys, girls and old men clutch swords, pluck on lutes and carry plates of food. These allegorical figures represent the likes of poetry, meditation and charity. Stone and tesserae complement each other beautifully.

Docklands Light Railway

A comparatively new line that sprang up around the redevelopment of the Docklands to serve the new skyscrapers around Canary Wharf, the Docklands Light Railway (DLR) opened in 1987 and has been extended piecemeal ever since; its southbound branches currently terminate at Lewisham and Woolwich Arsenal, while Stratford and Bank are the main London termini. Separate from the Underground, the tracks of this service look down on ground level for much of the journey. There are fewer tunnels and some fabulous views; away from the Victorian housing and Gothic steeples that dominate so much of London, gliding through Canary Wharf feels like a visit to Manhattan or Tokyo. Its chief novelty is that its trains are driverless: for train drivers, a grim portent of the future; for passengers, a rush to the front seats in the first carriage, where they can play at being the driver. Look out for a metal line running along the side of a building just outside West India Quay, where you cross the Meridian line dividing the Eastern and Western hemispheres.

WOOLWICH ARSENAL

ST GEORGE'S GARRISON CHURCH
Grand Depot Road, SE18

Famous for its dockyards, arsenal and barracks, today Woolwich is a poor but proud community licking the wounds of deindustrialization. Its peripheral status within London will change very quickly with Crossrail, making the station two stops from Canary Wharf and six from the West End. As people are lured to Woolwich, they will discover the odd gemstone among the Wimpy bars and turf accountants. The lively main square is blighted by Europe's biggest Tesco, but Woolwich Common has John Nash's Rotunda with its distinctive 'big tent' lead roof, as well as a listed 'ha-ha', a walled ditch that, without interrupting the view, prevented livestock wandering from common to barracks (the name indicated the mirth to be had watching unsuspecting ramblers fall in). The Edwardian town hall is one of the greatest in England, and the far end of Powis St has a pair of marvellous art-deco cinema buildings, now occupied by 'charismatic' churches (one of which, according to its website, inexplicably believes its building to be Gothic). Across the road from the Georgian barracks is a melancholy sight: the few surviving traces of the Royal Garrison Church of St George, a magnificent Byzantine/Romanesque church almost entirely destroyed by a V1 doodlebug in 1944. Seen from Woolwich New Rd, the unroofed walls of a shamrock-shaped chancel look like an old storage barn or obsolete industrial object. Through an exposed entrance arch, supported by pink marble columns with carved angels and griffins, you can see the chancel at the opposite end of a small garden where the nave used to be. There are some excellent mosaics. St George dispatches his dragon above the altar, and marble tablets on either side name Victoria Cross recipients from the Crimean War onwards. Tantalizing sepia photos on the internet show the original dimensions of the church and make the few scraps left to us seem an orphan. As the church itself is a victim of war, its amputated condition makes a poignant memorial for human victims.

LEWISHAM

THE CATFORD CAT
154 Rushey Green, SE6 4HQ

Admirers of Mikhail Bulgakov's satire *The Master and Margarita*, where the Devil visits Soviet Moscow with a human-sized, vodka-drinking black cat in tow, may feel like they have bumped into an old friend if they encounter the Catford Cat, plucky mascot for this unfashionable area south of Lewisham High St. The Catford shopping centre was built adjacent to the Broadway in 1974. A sign that extends out onto Rushey Green is barely legible because a giant fibreglass cat, ears and tail pricked up, crouches on top and paws at the sign's text. Catford appears to have taken its name from a ford over the Ravensbourne river, which was frequented by wild cats. A darker version of this story has the river used for the mass execution of black cats during witch trials; this is unlikely, as the name predates the fashion for witchhunting by several centuries. The rest of the area is an architectural dolly mixture: Eros House across the road is stern brutalism, the curving Broadway Theatre on the corner is an art-deco/Gothic hybrid, and the old dog stadium is being converted into (what else?) expensive flats. Like much of the surrounding area, the shopping centre has seen better days and its current form is unlikely to survive the mooted regeneration of Catford. It seems unthinkable that anyone would defy superstition and get rid of the cat.

GREENWICH

LIST OF BENEFACTORS, PAINTED HALL
Old Royal Naval College, King William Walk, SE10 9NN

The modern-day custom that sees sporting tournaments and art exhibitions sponsored by banking conglomerates may have its roots in the eighteenth century. Sitting serene by the river, Wren's Greenwich Hospital (now known as the Old Royal Naval College) is one of London's best-loved buildings. The briefing not to block the river view from Inigo Jones's Queen's House proved beneficial, as the green space between the twin domes carries the eye all the way up to Greenwich Observatory. Under the domes are the chapel and the Painted Hall, the latter by Sir James Thornhill, who also painted the interior of Wren's dome at St Paul's. Chocolate brown and gold are the main colours and they amplify the burst of light and colour in the box around the high table. Frolicking cherubs, nubile graces and quotations from Virgil advertise the wise governance of the Hanoverians. Around the entrance are three painted shields, flanked by angels and gesticulating boys, providing a tally of how much money each benefactor stumped up for the hospital, starting at £50 (the King comes first but is not the biggest donor). The names are laid out like the credits on an old Hollywood film. It seems vulgar to set out the sums like this (were they paying for the sailors to have this hall, or to have their names displayed?) but the results of the beneficence can only be applauded. As

Kenneth Clark put it: 'What is civilisation? A state of mind where it is thought desirable for a naval hospital to look like this, and for the inmates to dine in a splendidly decorated hall.'

GREENWICH FOOT TUNNEL
King William Walk, SE10 9HT

The bridges across the Thames enjoy the status of London icons, but there are other ways to cross the river. A piece of engineering from the heyday of London's docks, this tunnel for pedestrians was designed to get south Londoners to and from their jobs on the Isle of Dogs. The distinctive entrances can be found in Island Gardens and next to the Cutty Sark; twin red brick rotunda structures, topped by glass domes. A metal plaque on the Greenwich entrance marks the tunnel's opening in 1902. This end is accessed by a spiral staircase, the Isle of Dogs end by a lift. Fifty feet below the river, the tunnel itself is grubby and harshly lit, with blank tiles and cast-iron supports. There is no advertising, no cupcake stall, and no 'visitor experience'. In an age when public space is so heavily monetized, the tunnel simply gets people from A to B with a few minutes' silence to clear the head. It is a chill and airless place that pleases by making no effort to please. After the tourist hubbub of Greenwich, Island Gardens is quiet. It offers an excellent view of Wren's Greenwich Hospital that contrasts with the power station on its right flank.

QUEEN CAROLINE'S BATH
Greenwich Park, SE10 8QY

When the Prince Regent was crowned King George IV in 1821, his estranged wife Caroline of Brunswick was ordered to stay away from the ceremony. She flouted these orders and tried to enter Westminster Abbey through the East Cloister, West Cloister, Westminster Hall and Poets' Corner. All four doors were slammed in her face. This may sound mortifying, but Caroline was a woman for whom humiliation held no fear. George already had a few lovers, including a legally invalid Catholic wife, when he cleared his personal debts (£60 million in today's money) by marrying Caroline from the small German city-state now known as Braunschweig. They were introduced shortly before the wedding; finding a ribald motormouth who cared little for personal hygiene, George's first reaction was to walk to the other end of the room and call for a glass of brandy. The pair separated within a year and pursued promiscuous lifestyles. Rumours of Caroline having had a baby with her footman led to a 'Delicate Investigation' by senior politicians. She left the country, took a Milanese soldier as her servant/lover on a Mediterranean tour, and shocked society wherever she went, dancing topless and dressing like a young girl into her corpulent fifties. When George became king she returned to claim her place as queen consort but met her Waterloo at the abbey, dying a year later. Before her exile, Caroline had held an alternative court at Montague House, Greenwich, which

George later destroyed. All that remains are the steps into Caroline's bath, beneath ground level and set within a few patio slabs, which must have been the scene for many a boisterous party.

DEPTFORD BRIDGE

PETER THE GREAT
Deptford Creek, Glaisher Street, SE8

Stories about Peter the Great suggest that his absolute power allowed him to pursue sadistic tendencies, and exploit the scientific curiosity of the Enlightenment to satisfy his whims. He once forced his attendants to eat human flesh at a dissection. He was a keen amateur dentist, stopping courtiers at random and pulling out their teeth, often removing collateral chunks of gum; by the end of his life he had amassed a sackful. He also founded St Petersburg and his wide-ranging reforms transformed Russia from a medieval backwater into a modern, Westernized nation. One of his chief innovations was to make Russia a maritime power; to learn the ropes, he interrupted his reign with stays in the Netherlands and England, where he studied and practised shipbuilding. Spending a few months in Deptford in 1698, he rented Sayes Court from John Evelyn. By the time he moved out 300 window panes had been broken, twenty-five valuable paintings torn up, fifty chairs used for firewood, the curtains and bed linen shredded, and every floor coated in ink and grease. Wren was sent to survey the damage and recommended that Russia should compensate Evelyn to the tune of £350 (around £1 million today). This may explain why London did not get around to commemorating Peter's visit until 2001. Close to Greenwich on the riverfront, Peter's statue is as eccentric as the man himself. The six-foot-seven ruler's statue has a pinched, skinny look, suggesting that if our own statues derive from the Greco-Roman tradition, those of Russia are more influenced by Byzantine icons. Under a tricorne hat, Peter's head looks strangely tiny for his lanky frame. He holds a telescope and a pipe, and stands on a marble staircase, bordered along its rear by a balustrade and flanked by two cannon. To his left is an empty baroque throne; to his right is a dwarf in a matching frock coat, clutching a gyroscope.

CANNON BOLLARDS
The Colonnade, Grove Street, SE8 3AY

A good way to humiliate your vanquished adversary is to recycle their deadliest weapons, making them fulfil functions for which they were not devised. In Italy, Trieste has a large statue of Giuseppe Verdi made from melted-down Austrian guns. Britain set the armaments of Napoleon a more mundane task. When the Navy racked up its crucial victories in the Napoleonic wars, it inherited the French cannon on captured ships. The obvious thing was to fit them onto British ships but the prospect of all that lost business horrified British manufacturers, who successfully lobbied the government to scrap the guns. The solution reached was to employ the redundant cannon as traffic bollards, preventing entry into one-way or pedestrianized streets. This reminder of Trafalgar evidently tickled national pride, as bespoke bollards soon came to be based on the cannon design. There are a few cannon bollards left in London, including those on Grove St at the gates to an old victualling yard. Sunken into the pavement are a quartet of black guns, with the top segments painted white and, like the cherry on the cake, cannonballs stopping the muzzles. All that is left of the yard is a row of officers' houses, now called the Colonnade. The gateway's roundels feature pairs of crossed anchors. Today the area is a fairly remote corner of Deptford, dominated by Trellick-style blocks of municipal housing that, in their present run-down state, recall David Cameron's put-down to Tony Blair: 'He was the future once.'

SKULLS AND CROSSBONES
St Nicholas C of E Church, Deptford Green, SE8 3DQ

Christopher Marlowe is presented as an Elizabethan rock star, a Brian Jones of the South Bank. He is believed to have infiltrated the Stuart court as a government spy. His translation of Ovid's *Amores* was banned, and his plays feature fearless iconoclasts – Tamburlaine, the emperor who burns the Quran and declares himself 'scourge of God', or Dr Faustus, who scoffs that 'hell's a fable'. His work influenced Shakespeare and he died young, apparently killed in 1593 over a disputed bill at a Deptford inn. He was buried in an unmarked grave at Deptford's St Nicholas Church. There has been a church here since the twelfth century and the current building, in the nature of old churches, looks a composite from different periods. The red brick and broad round-topped windows are characteristic of City churches after the Great Fire, but the asymmetrical stone tower looks older. Its most striking feature is the skull and crossbones, sitting on the two posts of the churchyard entrance. St Olave Hart St in the City is famous for the grinning skulls above its gateway, but the Deptford skulls are much larger and more sinister, with gaping eye sockets. St Nicholas being patron saint of sailors, and Deptford a seafaring area, these skulls are thought to have inspired the Jolly Roger flag flown by eighteenth-century pirates. The skulls are a useful reminder that men are mortal, a fact upon which our age prefers not to dwell. The district's piratical associations came full circle in the 1990s when Captain Morgan rum (after Henry Morgan, who terrorized Spanish settlements in the Caribbean) was a shirt sponsor for Millwall FC. The church is on Deptford Green, a little north of Deptford Church St. Just off Church St is another church, St Paul's, built in the 1710s and a very handsome example of English baroque, with a rounded portico supporting a round tower and pointed steeple.

CROSSHARBOUR

POLYCHROME BRICKWORK
The Space, 269 Westferry Road, E14 3RS

The cringeworthy name of The Space theatre belies what is a striking and unexpected piece of architecture on Westferry Rd, the lengthy thoroughfare on the western edge of the Isle of Dogs. The last thing you expect to be hiding out amid the industrial estates, timid yellow-brick housing and Asian corner shops is a miniature, red-and-blue negative of Pisa Duomo; and yet there it is. Three round Romanesque arches form the entrance, with rows of nine, then five, smaller arches filling the rest of the façade and more running over the side windows. The trick of using contrasting colours to make humbug stripes is familiar from Siena or Orvieto, but in these arches the clash of dark blue with vermilion, thrown against brown brick walls, has a brasher effect. Both polychrome brickwork and Italian pastiche became fashionable in Victorian Britain. A famously garish example can be seen at the Templeton carpet factory on Glasgow Green, which impersonates the Doge's Palace in Venice. The Space was built in 1859 as St Paul's Presbyterian Church; today, the Scottish dockers who would have filled its pews are long gone and we can be grateful that thespians intervened to save it. The theatre's patron is Sir Ian McKellen and it presents an intelligent programme, from lesser-known Shakespeare to adaptations of literary favourites.

CANARY WHARF

HSBC LIONS
HSBC Bank, 8 Canada Square, E14 5HQ

The HSBC tower acts as right-hand lieutenant to the blinking pyramid atop Canary Wharf. It is all glass except for the sizeable logo on top, which puts its stamp onto the city as if it were a banking ledger. The Canary Wharf towers dominate the eastern skyline and can be seen from miles around. At the base of the HSBC tower, two great lions mark the entrance, standing guard over all those valuable numbers in a computer. These are replicas of the lions from the bank's original headquarters in the Far East. Today, the tentacles of HSBC have infiltrated every corner of the world; but knowing that it was originally the Hongkong and Shanghai Banking Corporation, you might expect to find Chinese lions with gurning faces, manes in stylized curls and paws resting on balls. You would be wrong; the bank was founded by Britons and its realistic lions are more Trafalgar Square than Gerrard St. The inspiration to place lions by the bank's entrance came from the Venetian Arsenale. Locals in Shanghai developed great affection for the lions, and passers-by would stroke them in the hope that some of that money might flow their way. One lion roars and bares its terrible fangs, the other remains watchful and pensive with pursed lips. The lions were named Stephen and Stitt, after the two Shanghai managers whose contrasting styles their postures appeared to reflect. In World War II, the Hong Kong lions were removed by the Japanese, who intended to melt them down. They were returned after being recognized by an American sailor in Osaka. The London lions were cast locally, at a foundry in nearby Limehouse, to mark the opening of the tower in 2002.

TRAFFIC-LIGHT TREE
Trafalgar Way, E14 5TG

On the roundabout outside Billingsgate fish market, which was moved from the City to Canary Wharf in 1982, drivers are strongly advised not to take heed of the lights. Branching out from a single post is a cacophony of seventy-five traffic lights, all jutting out at odd angles and continually flashing contradictory signals. This could prove most alarming to any motorist not expecting it. It is not, of course, intended to direct traffic, although were it in Tokyo you might think twice. Originally placed on Westferry Rd, the work replaced a plane tree that was unable to withstand the pollution. A competition was held and the winner was French artist Pierre Vivant, whose piece reflects the restless activity in the skyscrapers of Canary Wharf. Each light is on its own cycle, controlled by a computer; it was initially hoped that the lights would change to reflect movements on the stock exchange, but the cost was prohibitive. The traffic-light tree is regarded with affection, but its implications are disturbing. Nature is supplanted by the man-made; each set of lights is a competing voice, like those on the trading floors nearby, pushing its own agenda in a Darwinian struggle. We are overloaded with information to the point where we cannot digest it, and perceive only a wall of white noise.

POPLAR

STREETS IN THE SKY
Robin Hood Gardens, Woolmore Street, E14 0HG

Poplar High St is a strange and desolate place. There are a few good buildings, such as a Victorian college adorned with thistles and boys grabbing geese, but far fewer amenities than one might expect of a high street. It is oppressed on two fronts: by the skyscrapers of Canary Wharf, which cast a long shadow over the area, and by the hungry Blackwall Tunnel, a black hole whose gravitational pull seems to drain the surrounding streets of life. Kept apart from the high street by a ring of high walls and fences are the notorious Robin Hood Gardens. These twin housing blocks in concrete, ten storeys high and around 100 metres long, look as if they have been designed to punish residents. The architects, Alison and Peter Smithson, intended that long balcony walkways would serve as meeting places, or 'streets in the sky', preserving the communities that had been forged on the terraced streets that high-rises were replacing. The blue-collar workers for whom these flats were built did not want them; the Barbican and the Unités of Le Corbusier succeeded by acknowledging this. Peter Smithson later admitted the failure of the project, remarking that 'the week it opened, people would shit in the lifts, which is an act of social aggression.' When moves were initiated to have Robin Hood Gardens demolished, architectural luminaries such as Richard Rogers intervened.

A recurring argument attributes Robin Hood's failure to its use as a 'sink estate' to house problem tenants. Residents were consulted, and over 75 per cent gave their blessing to the demolition, but attempts to preserve the buildings continue.

LIMEHOUSE

HAWKSMOOR PYRAMID
St Anne's Church, Three Colt Street, E14 7HP

Mention the name Hawksmoor to a Londoner today and unless they are up on their architecture, they'll assume you are off to an upmarket steakhouse. Among connoisseurs, Nicholas Hawksmoor, assistant to Christopher Wren, still enjoys a certain cachet for his six-and-a-bit London churches. In the twentieth century he came to be seen as the bad boy of church builders; if Wren was the Beatles, Hawksmoor was the Stones. St Mary Woolnoth appeared in T. S. Eliot's *The Waste Land*; Ian Nairn compared this church to the experience of mescaline. In 1975 Iain Sinclair traced ley lines and pentagrams in the positioning of Hawksmoor's East End churches and satanic elements in their design. By the eighties Peter Ackroyd and Alan Moore were taking this notion to its logical conclusion and concocting grisly fiction in which the churches host

human sacrifices and direct the
deeds of Jack the Ripper. The
interior of Hawksmoor's churches
contradict the dark theories,
tending as they do towards blazing
bright baroque. His favoured
'box within a box' layout acts as
an intensifier, which Nairn saw
as Protestant rather than satanic
– although I can think of a few
people who would assert that

these are one and the same. St Anne's polygonal lantern
tower, with the Navy's white ensign fluttering above,
catches the eye from a distance, a shaking fist as you leave
the Isle of Dogs. One curiosity to set the imagination racing
is found in its churchyard: a four-sided stone pyramid, in
five segments and nine feet high, that has sat here since
1730. It is inscribed with 'The Wisdom of Solomon' in
reference to an apocryphal sacred text. As to why it sits
here, your guess is as good as mine. The most sensible
theory is that the pyramid was originally intended to
stand on or between the stumpy turrets at the east end of
the church, but the masons baulked at hoisting it up there.
Whether the Egyptian symbol seemed improper, or just
too heavy, is not recorded. Sinclair's *Lud Heat* contains
an alternative proposal that is frankly bonkers, but much
more fun.

STRATFORD

MARTYRS' MONUMENT, ST JOHN'S CHURCH
St John's Parish Church, Broadway, E15 1NG

The Reformation was one of the most chaotic and violent periods in European history. Breaking from Rome while remaining suspicious of Protestantism's more radical strains, the English adopted a centrist position that generally kept a lid on conflict, and yet some blood was spilt. During her five-year reign Mary I, daughter of Henry VIII and Catherine of Aragon, restored Catholicism as state religion. Her enthusiastic burning and exiling of Protestants earned her the sobriquet 'Bloody Mary'. These days, Stratford Broadway is eclipsed by the Newham-does-Dubai developments of the Olympic Park and Westfield shopping centre, but it still strives to perform the role of a traditional high street. The Broadway splits in two to snake around St John's Church, whose yard contains a Victorian memorial to local martyrs of Mary's persecution. These include a group of thirteen who were burnt together before crowds of 20,000. Tall and slender with an outsized spire like a dunce's cap, the six-sided memorial is in a cool pink terracotta, which renders more starkly the martyrs' perceived offences: 'preaching against auricular confession, transubstantiation, purgatory and images', or 'denying the corporeal presence of Christ's body and blood in the sacrament'. The memorial stands eighty-five-feet tall, but is camouflaged behind trees on a traffic island.

Acknowledgements

Thank you to . . .

Everyone at Michael O'Mara, in particular Hugh Barker for plucking me from obscurity, and my editor Gabriella Nemeth for adapting my jottings, with the help of the talented illustrator James Nunn, into such a stylish little book.

The many writers, living and dead, whose work I plundered for research and inspiration. Geoff Nicholson and Travis Elborough have been very kind and Chris Partridge's *Ornamental Passions* website has been an invaluable resource.

Readers of my blog, and all the friends who have encouraged my writing, especially Richard Boon, Andrew Chilton, Gareth Mulvenna, Johnny Vertigen and Giorgiana Violante.

My parents Terry and Joyce and my siblings Lydia and Natasha, for their love and support, and my partner Charlie, for making London such a fun place to be.

Index

INDEX

INDEX